NEXT 7 GENERATIONS WILL NEVER FORGIVE YOU

LET'S BE ULTRA RICH NOW

notionpress.com

NEXT 7 GENERATIONS WILL NEVER FORGIVE YOU

LET'S BE ULTRA
RICH NOW

AVINASH
SISODE

notionpress
.com

Notion Press

Old No. 38, New No. 6
McNichols Road, Chetpet
Chennai - 600 031

First Published by Notion Press 2016

ISBN 978-93-5206-880-7

मुख्य मंत्री
महाराष्ट्र

सत्यमेव जयते

Chief Minister
Maharashtra

20th May 2016

MESSAGE

I am happy to learn that Mr. Avinash Sisode is bringing out his book 'Next 7 Generations Will Never Forgive You'

It is the need of the society to become financially stable and lead a more prosperous life and make a difference in this world. It makes me happy that youth like Avinash Sisode is actively participating in this process.

I hope that this book will help young entrepreneurs from Maharashtra to start their business and establish themselves as a job givers.

I congratulate Mr. Avinash Sisode for this initiative and extend my best wishes for his future initiatives.

(Devendra Fadnavis)

Testimonial

Mr Avinash Sisode wrote this book so that you can write yours. A superb demonstration of how you can transform an ordinary life into an extraordinary success story through the 7 Sutras Mentioned in this Book. For the Aspiring & Budding enterpreneurs this shall serve as an excellent Motivational Tool.The book has my highest recommendations especailly with reference to Generation Next.

Ashok M Katariya (Chairman Ashoka Buildcon)

If you are looking for a book which can guide you from rags to riches...this is it... Avinash and got into the psychology of every lower-middle class dreamer and shown the journey of transformation to a successful businessman beautifully in this book. A must read for every Indian.

Rajiv Talreja (International Bestseller Author – Lead or Bleed)

It is such a great and interesting jounery of such a hard working person. I have truly become a big Fan of him.This is such a great book. By reading this book only one thing I can tell is that "Never tell your destination where the hurdles are, But always tell your hurdles your destination.

Bhavesh Bhatia (Blind Entrepreneur and Founder of Sunrise Candles)

A very gripping book “Next 7 generations will never forgive you”

I have just completed the book in two sittings. The whole conversation is in such a simplistic way, without any jargons and communicates very serious management techniques.

I find the book very inspiring for any entrepreneur. Opens up the complete pathway for the person to take on the business with confidence.

It’s a very rare book to give practical simple route to success.

S.R. Swamy

Former CEO Kalyani Global Engineering

Center Director Indo European Educational Services Pvt. Ltd

Dedicated to my adorable son Lakshya.....

Your arrival and presence in my and your mother

Suvarna's life is the real inspiration behind this book....

About the Author

Mr. Avinash Sisode was born in a small village having population of less than 1000 people, about 200 kms from Mumbai, India. Though born in a farmer family and brought up in a village, Avinash Sisode, at the age of tweny-two knew that his entrepreneurial dreams were about to take flight. He is keen to share these experiences with entrepreneurs to motivate them to start their own business. The true defining moment in Avinash Sisode's life was the start of the company E & G. The E & G Group currently has a portfolio of 9 different companies under it which includes a couple of startups to real estate mavericks in their industry domain. This Group's success is largely based on Avinash Sisode's business model and under his leadership. Avinash Sisode believes that his life's mission is to spread love, joy and prosperity in the world. His passion in life is to create, support and nurture entrepreneurs. Avinash has successfully empowered more than 100,000 people by changing their mindset. He has helped them in personality development, teaching how to connect their passion to a sustainable business module and even taught them to build and present their business plans to potential investors.

"Together we can create miracles" is his motto.

Contents

Preface

The most common misconception in the world is that being wealthy and successful is related to intellect, only hard-work, and also being lucky. But, being wealthy is neither an intellectual exercise nor it is only hard-work. It requires the ability to think and act in a certain way. Look at the wealthy people around you. Are they really well-educated or very hard-working? The answer more than often is no, yet we see them parade around town in luxury and make us wonder what is their story to success. However, the one uniting link between all wealthy people is that they are financially literate. They know how to make money work for them and not the other way around. That is the reason, they sustain their wealth. Financial literacy is the key to sustainability. Ask yourself, whether you earn money every day and sustain it for long. If your answer to the first question is 'yes' and to the second is 'no,' then you really need to be financially literate.

This book addresses those very points that harbor on the knowledge of financial literacy. Here we follow the story of simple man named Ravi who wants to be able to live a comfortable life. However, there are adverse factors against his current financial situation however we see the earning to become rich and successful someday. That is when Ravi meets the Wealth-Guru, a man that has been the guiding light for many successful entrepreneurs.

The Wealth-Guru has various sutras that help Ravi understand the true meaning of wealth. Ravi learns how to create abundance in his life. Wealth means money, success, happiness, abundance and fame and it is gaining this wealth on which Ravi embarks his journey. We come to know that we too can live a full-fledged life if we are wealthy. Rich people can erase the word 'compromise' from their dictionary. One can visit many countries and buy anything. One can own many precious and rare things, because money gives choices and access.

This book also addresses the social issue of poverty. Poverty is still a prevalent situation in our country. However, it is the understanding the poverty and mediocrity is the true problem behind a backward society. Many people think that being rich is a crime. Most people fail to change this very perception of theirs and spend a life in mediocrity.

It is known that our country was at the helm of prosperity for the world 200 years ago. That means, our tradition teaches us to be rich and peaceful. And it is the ultimate fulfillment of life. It is in our core values as a society to be able to lead a very wealthy life yet we find ourselves shying away from this very sense of fulfillment.

If we want to make our country a financial super-power in the coming decade, we need to make this country the "entrepreneur's capital" of the world. It is indeed fulfilling to see more and more young people taking an interest in creation and show the need to want to live a life of abundance. The overall scenario shows that the current generation is inclining towards becoming wealthy and living a life of abundance. Ravi's story in life is centric around this very idea.

The idea of abundance lies in the acknowledgement of creating enough wealth that will last 7 generations. What difference does it make whether your previous or future generations are wealthy or not? 'You becoming ultra-rich for next 7 generations' is a call that we all must make to live a fulfilled life. What exactly is 'becoming ultra-rich?' there is an infinite wealth in the universe. It remains infinite even if you take infinite wealth from it. Owning that infinite wealth is becoming ultra-rich. This is the ultimate goal.

This book contains important guidelines to becoming ultra-rich. Come then, turn the pages and let s start a great revolution; a great journey to become ultra-rich for the next 7 generations.

Acknowledgements

To all the E&G directors, who are always supportive to my every new expedition.

To Mrs. Mukta Deshpande for editing this book.

To my team: Poonam, Pravin, Supriya, Shubham, vardhan.

To my dear friend Zakir who kept the possibility of writing a book consistently alive.

To my mentor Mr. T. R. Doongaji for his consistent guidance.

To all my family members.

Chapter 1

I can't be Rich

It was a beautiful winter morning. A mild breeze was blowing across the garden. The blossoming garden was basking in the glorious morning sun. The lush green lawn was inviting me to sit outside and have a cup of tea. I was tempted to do so, as it was Sunday, a day off from daily routine. I was eager to fill my lungs with the fresh air and fragrance of my blooming roses, adjacent to the lawn. I was about to ask Gopal, my butler cum house keeper to bring tea, when the doorbell rang. I opened the door and there stood a very handsome and well dressed couple with two kids. The kids too, were smartly dressed. The gentleman was wearing an Armani outfit. He was wearing specs through which his eyes were gleaming in delight. I had seen him somewhere but could not remember. The lady, his wife I presumed, was very elegant, wearing a long skirt and a blouse certainly from a much renowned fashion house. She was clearly not of Indian origin, as she was a blonde. I saw a Rolls Royce, and a Maybach parked on the main road. I was wondering who the guests might be; still I greeted them and beckoned them to come inside.

While they were entering, I was scratching my brains to identify these visitors. It took me almost a minute to recognize the gentleman… What a transformation!! "Ravi!" I exclaimed. "What a pleasant surprise! Where were you all these years? No contact, no communication? Come dear! Come inside and have a seat."

All of them settled down on the sofa. I called my wife and my son and introduced them to Ravi. Ravi also introduced his wife Angel, who was a Spaniard, his son Vardhan and daughter Jolly. I was still wondering what made Ravi approach me after so many years. I asked him, "Where were you Ravi? We did not have any contact after our last meeting, though I was watching you on television, in newspapers and magazines frequently."

Ravi smiled; his eyes were twinkling with the joy of meeting someone dear after a long time. He said, "First of all; let me ask you, how are you? And please accept this small gift from us." He handed me a parcel. I was so excited to see him that I put the parcel aside to see it later. Ravi said, "Angel and I had decided to meet you only when I would have established my own business empire, as I had promised you during our last meeting. Today, I think I have achieved that position I had dreamt of; so here I come."

I was watching this gentleman with amusement… What a drastic change! Before me sat a very successful businessman, brimming with confidence! I have met many persons as a Wealth Guru, but this was a real surprise for me. This was the same man I had come across sixteen years ago, but with a completely different personality. Meanwhile, Gopal had brought tea and biscuits and served all of us. I was very eager to know how this change came about. I said to Ravi, "Please tell me more about yourself."

He started, "Now I am settled in Amsterdam and I am doing a wonderful business there."

"That is great, Ravi!" I said.

Sipping the tea, Ravi just looked at me and said, "Sir, do you remember? Sixteen years back I had come to meet you?"

The glimpses of the past flashed in my mind. "Yes, I do remember. You had come to me with the reference of your Yoga student. I still remember your looks and your body language, as you came in."

I looked at Ravi's face. He was completely engrossed in the past memories. He continued, "It was a sunny morning in May. That first time, we met at your home. I still remember your living room, Sir. The first thing that struck me was the hugeness of your house in Rajasthani style, or let me call it a mansion: a well-maintained garden and the polished mahogany main door. I glanced with awe at the two Mercedes, parked in the porch. When I was ushered inside the house by your butler, I looked around in wonder… At the rich Persian rugs covering the floor, curios and souvenirs from various countries arranged tastefully on the mantelpiece, fresh flowers from the garden placed in the porcelain flower-vases, heavy curtains covering the French windows, the choicest and the most famous works of Raja Ravi Varma, da Vinci and Michelangelo displayed on the walls. The color scheme of that spacious room was soothing to the eyes and warm and welcoming. One could instantly feel the air of hospitality."

I smiled at the detailed description. Ravi had a sharp memory, I thought. He took a deep breath and said, "At that time, I was struggling in life, managing family and finances. Nothing worked for me. My Yoga student told me that I should meet this man that is you, Sir. You are a Wealth Guru, he said. He told me that you are a very successful entrepreneur with diversified businesses. Your passion is to create, support and nurture entrepreneurs. You are someone who would coach and guide me to build business, to become rich. He told me that you are the man responsible for guiding so many people in their lives and they have become rich, ultra-rich by following your guidance. Many people have started businesses and created fortunes under your mentoring. That is why I came to you. I had an image in my mind and I was nervous. But, surprisingly you made me comfortable with your warmth and kindness, Sir. You offered me a cup of tea. We started talking. And the very first question I asked was, 'Can anybody become rich?'"

"Yes. That was the first question you asked Ravi. And I replied, 'Yes! Anybody can become rich by following a certain way,'" I recalled.

That May morning stood before my eyes vividly... Ravi had just looked at me with a totally different expression on his face and bluntly asked me, "Sir, is it possible for anybody to be rich?" I had again replied emphatically, "Yes Ravi, anybody can be rich if he follows a certain way."

Ravi was thinking about what I was saying. He started to digest the sentence slowly. He said, "Anybody can be rich, but I can't."

I was astonished and I asked, "Why are you saying so?"

Ravi said, "I am from a very poor family. I have asked my parents and grandparents and they have convincingly told me that we can't be rich because from our last seven generations, we are the poorest in the society. Nobody in our family has attained any remarkable achievement. As we belong to the most backward class of the society of this country, we can't become rich. Also, there were so many mouths in the family to feed. We are four brothers and three sisters, my father being the only earning member and the caretaker of the family. And now, I have started working after completing my education. The salary I receive by working day and night, including over-time, is not sufficient even to feed the whole family. My grandfather was an 'Ayurvedacharya', he had taught me Yoga and some treatment modalities. I have tried that as well. I used to take morning Yoga classes and used to give treatment for minor ailments; but it is also not making much earning. So, there is no way to think about any enjoyment and entertainment. We are in hand to mouth situation."

Ravi took a deep breath. I offered him a glass of water. He gulped it down and continued, "That is how we are surviving. How can I become rich? Now, I have come to the conclusion that only certain people, who are from the upper class of the society, the children of business people and some big bureaucrats, can be rich. People like me cannot be rich at all. I can clearly see the future now. I come from the slum area. Everybody around me is poor. The highest level of richness that only a few amongst us have experienced is having a motorbike. And my condition is so worse that I can't even dream about a motorbike. Some of my relatives doing reputed jobs in big cities often say that we can only make ends meet. We can never be rich. When I look around, I can see people, who are very poor. There are very few people who are rich in this society and this town. Wherever I look, I see only poverty and destitution. There is nothing much to achieve in life. This is what I have seen in the movies too. The hero is a very poor guy. He marries the heroine who is a rich girl and so become rich. Apart from this, I have not seen a single way to become rich. In some movies, the hero rides a bicycle first and it flashes on the screen 'after seven years'... finally the hero gets out of his Mercedes. I don't understand what happened in between. Nobody has shown me that. This is the reality, Sir. In movies, people who are rich are either smugglers or builders. They become rich by destroying slum areas with bulldozer and unethical activities. I can't do such things, Sir. So, I find no other way to become rich."

Here was a man, on the verge of breaking down completely. I had come across many struggling men and women, but this one was so much in mental distress that I felt very sorry for him and decided to listen to him patiently, without interrupting. He continued, "I had come to the conclusion that the only way become rich is to marry a rich girl. But Sir, look at me! Who will marry me? So, now I have decided not to marry at all and not to have kids. Why should I? As my past seven generations have experienced poverty, I cannot put my future generations in the same conditions."

"I am clear that, there is no simple or ethical way of becoming rich. The ways that I have come across are either unethical or illegal or criminal. I am a God-fearing person and I will not do any sinful activity in my life."

The Wealth Guru inside me was now taking command of the situation. I asked, "Ravi, can you think of any other way of becoming rich?"

"Yes Sir," he replied. "If you give me lots of money, I can be rich. Because it takes money to make money and I don't have a single penny to do anything, or to invest or create new money. As I don't have money how can I be rich?

I have seen some people in my community. They have attempted to do different things, but they failed. This fear of failure always nags me. If I attempt something different and fail, what people will say? It is not that I had not thought of doing anything; as a matter of fact , many a times I had discussions with my friends about starting a business, but every time I dropped that idea out of fear of failure. I am always concerned about what people will say. What will my relative or my family members say? What will people in my area say? They will blame me. Failure is a very dangerous thing, Sir. All these thoughts make me depressed. So, it is better not to even think about becoming rich. What I believe is that God is playing a major role in making me poor. It is His wish, so what can I do? It is my destiny. If I am destined to be poor, how can I alter it? It is as simple as that, isn't it Sir? I have been talking for a long time now. Sir, please say something."

Ravi took a long pause. He looked at me with pleading eyes. I said, "Good Ravi! I am listening to you carefully. While you were speaking, I was going through your entire thought processes and such conversations are familiar to me; don't worry about what I will say or think. Keep talking whatever comes to your mind. So, you were talking about God's wish! What else?"

Ravi was much relaxed after my assurance. He said, "Whenever I start thinking about getting rich and starting business, the first thing that comes to my mind is, will people listen to me? They might ask, what experience do I have? I have only heard about business, but I don't know how to do it and exactly what business to do.

I don't know anything about it because; in my childhood days nobody in my school taught me such things. I didn't even know whether there are any educational programs related to business or any training about handling money. Not even my parents or relatives taught me such things. Till date, I have only heard about handling money that, "money doesn't grow on trees, or it takes money to make money. Money is the root of evil. Money is bad. We cannot earn more money by ethical ways. You have to do lots of illegal things to become rich. If you want to be happy, be poor." Right now, we are happy people, Sir. I don't want to mess up with the happiness of my brothers, sisters and parents. If I become rich, they will become unhappy, so it is better to be poor.

What I have observed is that money comes with sleepless nights, illness, and bad habits. I don't wish to invite all these things, so it is better to be poor. It is the only way of living a good life. God wants me to live a good life."

The dejected young man sat before me with his head hanging low in despair. I asked him softly, "Ravi, then why did you come here?"

He said, "Because my student sent me to you. He said, you are the one who will guide me in becoming rich."

I looked straight into his eyes smiling, and said, "It means, Ravi, that you want to be rich, and that is why you are here, and 'can anybody become rich, Sir?' was your first question. It means, you are still thinking about how to be rich."

"Yes Sir, I wish I could be, but I can't be rich."

He was cooling down a bit after boiling over his situation in life. I had many experiences of this kind in the past and knew that now he was ready to take in whatever advice I had to give him. It is always better to let people pour out the feelings and emotions choking up inside them, before I start talking. Now, this was the ideal moment for me to take control of the situation. I said, 'Okay, fine! Why don't we have a cup of tea?' I asked for tea and cookies for both of us. Taking a sip, I said, "Ravi, I really appreciate your sincere and authentic sharing. Now, I know your entire situation. What I liked most about you is, you still have a strong desire to be rich. Let us see, against all odds, why you shall be rich!"

Chapter 2

Why Shall I be Rich

"Yes Ravi," I repeated. "As a Wealth Guru, I am telling you this. We will see why you shall be rich; AND you can be rich! You have all those fighting abilities against poverty and a tough disposition, but you are not mentally prepared to come forward and face the situation. You are not feeling rebellious about your situation."

Ravi said, "Sir, I am totally confused by what you said right now. I am here because I want to be rich and you are saying that I don't intend to. I can't get you."

"Let me explain, Ravi," I continued. "You say that you don't want to be poor; but at the same time you love to live in this condition like the poor, because the poor get sympathy from others, from the family members and the society. They avoid taking responsibility as it takes efforts to alter any kind of situation. They like to stay in their comfort zone and put blame on destiny for everything. The poor love to get some subsidy or charity from the society, from the rich people, from the government.

But, the first and the foremost thing required is to challenge poverty, stand there firmly as a fighter and bring a shift in your thinking. Because, the way you think and the way you act, make you either poor or rich.

It is easy to blame destiny, but YOU choose to be poor or rich. You have chosen poverty, as you were talking about your last seven generations – your last seven generations have chosen poverty. So, look at the impact of poverty on your lives – you have not been able to get the education you have wanted or the food that you want to eat or the medical aid you deserve. You are dreaming of a better lifestyle. When you walk on the footpath, you see people wearing clothes you cannot buy, and eating food that you want to eat. You look through those shop windows and see people buying the things you want to have… You look at them and blame your destiny again and again. It will definitely influence your level of satisfaction, fulfillment and happiness. Poverty is a big malaise in our country. The criminal rate amongst children is increasing due to this; so is child labor. Why is there child labor? If the child does not work, he doesn't get food, and so children develop bad habits. They are deprived of good education. They easily fall prey to drugs, gambling, smoking and drinking. All this happens because of poverty.

You have chosen to live in poverty, you and your family. It is not the wish of God as you put it, or your destiny.

You say, God chose poverty for you. But, look at Nature. Nature is the biggest Guru, I think. How is Nature? It GROWS. There is growth in Nature. There is abundance. There is advancement and increase. We are also a part of Nature. We were created by God or Nature, like the plants and the animals. So, it is our birthright to grow. It is inherent in us, to develop, and it is our fundamental responsibility to make advancement and money. Being a human being, it is your principal commitment to yourself to earn more and increase your wealth, creating more assets. This is the real destiny for which God has created us. God never gives poverty and riches. He has given equal abilities to all human beings. It is your will to convert those abilities into reality that makes the difference.

All human beings live and die one day. Each one of us has a choice how to complete the journey in between. If all of us are going to die one day, then why not die rich? Because, the rich have choices. If I have ample money, I can visit distant lands. I can travel all over the world. I can even go into space and enjoy the journey. I can dive deep into the sea and see the wonders there. I can buy wonderful clothes and I can look good. I can eat what I want. I can buy a car or many cars of my choice. I can experience luxury.

You said, you don't want to create future generations because you are poor. That is why you are opting not to marry, right? The rich have choices. Money gives choices and abundance of money gives more choices. Only the rich can erase the poverty from this world, because they are the inspiration for the poor. You say that you really want to do something for the society and the community you come from. So, why not become rich and be a real role model for them? It has nothing to do with caste, religion or education. All this is created in our minds because you are thinking in the context of poverty."

Ravi was sitting before me, eagerly listening to what I was saying. I sensed that his mind was now like wet soil, ready to be sown with the seeds of new thoughts.

"Okay Ravi," I said, "You have been listening for a long time. Listening is one of the important abilities that you have developed – you learn to listen and think in a certain way. Thinking in a certain way is of immense value. It helps you to understand ways and methods of doing things. What we are sharing, discussing and talking with each other right now is of utmost importance.

Listen to me carefully. Only thinking will not make any difference in your life. After thinking, you will have to start acting in a certain way and that will definitely give you some results. So, here I want you to learn the way you must act. Let me tell you about two domains. One is being poor and the other is being rich. Under these two domains, there are various important aspects, and one of them is language. The language of a poor person is different from the language of a rich person. The poor will always say, 'I can't afford it, I can't do it, I will never get it, it is not good. Everything is about destiny.' And the rich will say, 'Yes, I can do it. Let me see, how I can afford it. Let me do that, let me do it along with my team.' They talk about team, they talk about abundance. They say, 'It is my destiny to be rich.' They say, 'I am God's expression. So, it is my fundamental responsibility to be rich.' This is the language of the rich. Compare this with your language. Not only the language, but if you look at any rich person you can observe the difference in his way of walking, talking and his level of confidence. So, let us consider the point, why people become rich.

The rich know they cannot use all the wealth they make – they create jobs; they contribute to the GDP of the nation. In my view, they are the real patriots who contribute to the country's progress. So, it can be said that, the way the rich speak and present themselves, is the language of their wealth.

Are you getting my point Ravi? The poor always work hard and the rich always work smart. They use smart ways of generating wealth. They know the various quadrants as Robert Kiyosaki has mentioned in his book (Rich Dad Poor Dad).

Creativity is also impaired when one is poor. The poor think in a linear way. And the rich think more creatively about the transformational way, about the way of living life and generating wealth. They are the visionaries who create their future, but the poor let themselves be victimized by their situation, the circumstances that they find themselves in and the people around them. On the contrary, the rich live the life they wish to lead. And they do this by acting in a certain way. Basically, it is a process. Do you understand? It is good that we are talking about it, Ravi. I know that it is impossible to live like a millionaire instantly, but at least you can look like one. That is the very first step to walk on this pathway. And it is not very difficult for a youngster like you to look like a millionaire. One day you will find yourself in the millionaire class of the society.

Once you are rich, people get to know you. More and more people recognize you. More and more people want to meet you. You become a personality; you become an idol for others. So, you have to think like a millionaire. Yes Ravi, it all begins with the thinking process."

Ravi sat there watching me silently, and then he said, "Yes, now I am getting you more clearly. It is all about the thinking process. It is so mind-numbing, all the conversation we have had so far. I am exhausted. Sir, please give me two to three days to think over it and I will come back to you."

I bid good bye to him and closed the door. Outside the Sun was now blazing in its full glory. I was sure that my words had penetrated through the darkness that had engulfed Ravi's mind and thought-process. He would definitely come back again.

As expected, Ravi returned after three days. We sat in the in the living room. He started talking, "Sir I have barely slept for two to three hours during the last three nights. Your words were going round and round in my head. I was unable to sleep. Whatever sleep I got I had dreams of money, money and money. Now, I have decided that I will become rich no matter what. It is simple. I will think about it and I will become rich."

He paused for a while and then continued, "I have an idea Sir and it will make me rich."

"Then tell me what is it Ravi," I said, amused by his resolution.

He said, "No Sir, it is my idea. You are a businessman and if I share my idea with you, you may start the same business. I will not share this with anyone, I will start working on it and within six months, I shall be rich. My idea is very unique; very few people have implemented such an idea."

I was keenly observing Ravi's enthusiasm. I cautioned him, "Ravi, the path is long and you have to go step by step towards your goal. Business and money are sensitive issues, so the whole process requires a lot of financial literacy as well as management. So, I request you that we shall meet again in a few days and I will discuss with you the pathways of success. I have so many ideas Ravi! Only one idea is not sufficient."

Ravi was already floating in the dream of becoming rich. He did not pay much attention to my words. He said hastily, "I am clear in my mind. So, why waste time? I want to start today! I will come back to you only when I become rich." He took my leave and disappeared!

Chapter 3

Great Haste Makes Great Waste

One year had passed. Another summer came. The memories of Ravi's visit were fading from my mind as I was busy meeting and consulting with many people during that year as a Wealth Guru. I had my tea early in the morning on that particular day. The heat was already increasing outside. The door bell rang exactly at 9 o'clock. This was the same time a year earlier when Ravi had called. I opened the door and there he was, a dejected young man, his shoulders drooping, standing at the doorstep. I was pleased to see him and said, "Welcome Ravi! What a pleasure to see you! Come inside and have a seat." We sat on the sofa. When he settled himself, I asked him where he was the whole year and what he was doing, as there was no communication between us. Ravi took a deep breath. He was clasping and unclasping his hands nervously. He said in a feeble voice, "Sir, please don't ask me! What you were telling me at that time was right. It really requires a lot of home-work to succeed. Now, I have realized that."

"Ravi, please explain yourself more elaborately, I don't understand what you are talking about," I said.

Ravi explained, "When I took your leave last year, I had said that I would make money by using my idea within six months."

I said, "Yes Ravi, I do remember. Now, can you tell me what that idea of yours was, which you didn't share with me earlier? I hope there is no need of secrecy now? I think you are ready now to share this idea of yours with me!"

Ravi smiled sheepishly, "Sir, why are you embarrassing me? Actually, every entrepreneur thinks that his or her idea is the best idea in the world. Basically, my idea was very simple. When I was a child, I used to observe my grandmother (mother's mother), my Nani, selling an Ayurvedic hair oil. At that time, she would follow one very simple tradition. She would sell that oil only on Saturdays. I didn't know the exact formula for making it at that time, but it would take the whole week to prepare the oil and then she would sell it on Saturday. Whenever I would visit her house on that day, I saw people standing in a long queue and demanding a liter or more oil; some wanted more than that."

"Everybody wanted that hair oil because it was so magical. After applying it on the head, any bald person could grow hair! It was the magical formula of my grandma. I had seen that Saturday rush with my own eyes. Then, when she was counting her last days, she passed on that formula to her children. My mother also knows it. But as you know, due to poverty and the responsibility of many children, she had kept away all that stuff, the formula and the ingredients for making it. Nowadays, many types of bottled hair oils are available in the market, so no one is interested in buying home-made hair oil. I know that formula is magical. No other hair oil claims to cure baldness totally. This was my secret idea. I was not ready to share it with you for this reason."

"Okay, okay Ravi that is fine! Now I understand your wish for secrecy! But what happened after that? Tell me."

"I thought it was as simple as this," Ravi began. "After taking your leave last year, I had this idea in mind. I thought I would just implement that. I would make tons of money and come back to you as I had promised and stand before you as a rich man! This was my simple business plan."

I was eager to know what happened next and asked him so. Ravi continued, "I went home and asked my mother about the formula. She said that we have to put certain Ayurvedic herbs into the mixture of coconut oil and sesame oil. She also told me the name of a very secret herb that I will not tell you right now. That herb would be mixed in the oil as well. I am very fond of Naturopathy and Ayurveda. I believe that Ayurveda is the best available therapy on this planet that can cure any disease from its roots and increases vitality of man. That is why I admire Ayurveda. It is a long story, Sir but I will make it short for you."

Ravi took a pause and I offered him a glass of water. He further continued his very interesting narrative, "This was my idea regarding the hair oil. I instantly decided to produce the oil on large scale and sell it all over India. I thought I would make my oil the top-selling brand in India. I shared my plan with a few of my friends and with some people doing export business. They promised me to export the oil to the European, American and South American countries. Then, assured by my friends and the people involved in the export business, I thought about the production. As I have told you, the formula of my grandma is a secret one; I was not ready to outsource the production, as some of the friends suggested. I was afraid that people would copy it. I decided to start my own factory. I went to some of my cousins, who were also aware of the formula and had seen the long lines at grandma's place. They encouraged me by saying that this idea would sell like anything. They lent me considerable money. Some of them asked for interest over it. I promised to return their money with interest. Then I purchased a plot in the industrial area and started the factory, took quotations from the vendors also. During this process, my budget started to bulge. There were certain issues that I had overlooked in my haste and enthusiasm. They popped up suddenly."

I was nodding silently. This was the typical case of an inexperienced and over-enthusiastic entrepreneur! Ravi was engrossed in his narration, "Sir, actually, I was planning for a small capacity plan, but my chartered accountant and people from some Govt. organization said that a bigger size plant would be better. I cancelled the orders for the first plant. Thus, I lost about 25 per cent of my money. I changed the first vendor and purchased advanced machinery from another. It was an Italian company.

Meanwhile, many things happened that I am not telling you, in case you get bored of my story."

"Okay Ravi," I said, "What happened next?"

"After facing many obstacles, the production started. There were natural calamities during that period, some management issues and shortage of funds. These things affected the work hugely."

"All this happened in the span of four months. I am a result-oriented person, Sir. I want quick results. But, the things didn't work well and the people around me were not good. This happened because of the circumstances and the people. There was no fault of mine... My life has come to a standstill because of these factors. I find myself in the adverse conditions now."

A year had passed since this young man had met me, but his mindset was the same. He was blaming the circumstances and people around him. I encouraged him to talk further.

He continued, "As I have told you, the oil was the secret formula of my grandma. It became a hit instantly. I have brought two bottles for you. You can try this. I was handling the production and sales, was raising funds, meeting people, negotiating with vendors. I was working day and night. In fact, I had built a guest house in the factory premises and I spent my days and nights there."

"All this sounds fine, Ravi. Then what was the problem? What exactly happened?" I asked. I wanted to hear the root cause of the problem he was trying to convey.

"Sir, the production was in full speed. The godown was full in the very first month. The machinery was excellent, so the production was very fast. I had to stop the production. I started selling through small vendors. Sir, I realized that producing is easier than selling a product! One day, one of my cousins told me about a distant relative. He was one of the big distributors of pharmacy products, mostly Ayurvedic, in North Maharashtra. I went to meet him and explained about my product. He was very kind towards me and listened patiently. He was ready to take my oil for selling as a wholesale distributor. He said that he would sell it across India. But, he put forward a condition. He asked me for a credit for three months. He promised to make payment in 90 days and I agreed."

"He offered me a good price, so I finalized the deal with him. We shook hands. The thought of making the deal legal or any written format never occurred to me, as he was a distant relative. I started supplying him. He organized our family get-together, so there was no doubt in my mind about his intentions. Then he organized two more programs; one with my community members and one with the people of my caste. They felicitated me there. I was so happy! Everything was sailing smoothly. We started working in two shifts to increase the production. All was well."

Now, I began to see what exactly might have happened. I almost knew it from my experiences with various people. Still, I wanted to hear the whole story from Ravi, as I knew very well that when people repeat their stories or tell them to a third person, they themselves realize their mistakes and it is easy to guide them after that. I beckoned to Ravi to continue.

"When the 90 days credit period was over, I went to him and asked for the payment. He said, "Wait for fifteen more days. I will call you myself and make your payment as I receive it from my customers." I waited again for fifteen days, because I trusted him. He had advised me not to stop the production, as he told me the oil was really wonderful."

"I went to him after waiting for two weeks. He assured me with his sweet words like before and gave me a small amount. I was astonished to see the meager amount, because I had produced and given him the oil that had cost me a billion rupees. I told him so. He calmed me down with his sweet tongue again. "Take this for the time being and come again in two weeks," he said." The same pattern was repeated over the next three months.

Many developments occurred during this period. More than two dealers complained against the product. They said the oil was not good and it was creating problems."

"And what were the problems?" I asked.

"They said that people were complaining of itching all over the scalp, and red eyes, after they used the oil. Two customers filed complaints against me in the police station. They also went to the Medicine Board of India to make a complaint."

I interrupted Ravi, "When this happened, what was your relative doing? What was his stand?"

"This so-called Mamaji of mine said, "See, this is how your oil is! Many of my dealers and customers are complaining against it. I have to think over our deal before I pay you. I cannot make your payment until this matter is settled." He cheated me Sir!"

I had expected as much!

Ravi continued, "But Sir, I had to pay my suppliers for the raw material. I had no money. As I had already taken loans from banks, I had no option but to seek help from the private sector. I went to a financier in our town. He gave me money."

"And it became the practice. I started going to the private money-lenders. The first financier gave me money with 1.5 per cent monthly interest. This amount vanished within two days! Then I went to another financier. He charged 2 per cent interest. I slowly realized that I had become a victim of this vicious circle. Finally, I borrowed money at 5 per cent monthly interest. This person is now at my throat, Sir! He has become a huge problem in my life, I can't pay him and

I can't run away from him, like we say in Hindi...'Gale mei atki haddi, nigal bhi nahi sakte aur thook bhi nahi sakte'".

"What is the amount that you took from him?" I asked. "I took 25 lacs at 5 per cent monthly interest. Now, it has amounted to 65 lacs!" Ravi explained.

"That is huge money for you Ravi!" I said.

"Yes Sir," Ravi said, "and now I don't know how to handle this situation. I took this money from Shripal Chowdhary. He is an infamous don of our area. He is threatening me now by saying that if I do not pay his money within a week, he will shoot me. My head is spinning and I don't know what to do. I am not able to sleep since last two weeks. I have no appetite left to eat anything. Life has become meaningless for me. Sometimes, I think about taking an extreme action; but the love of my parents and siblings pulls me back from taking rash action. I am helpless and that is why I have come here to seek your advice."

I rose and went to him. I patted on his back. Tears were almost rolling down his cheeks. He was the complete picture of wreckage.

I said to him in a calm and soothing voice, "Ravi, please calm down. Compose yourself. All people face such situations in their lives once in a while; you are not the only one. I have also gone through very trying circumstances myself. You might feel that this is life's end, but it is not so. There is always a breakthrough. There is always a ray of light at the end of every tunnel. So, don't lose hope. When you lose hope, you lose everything! Compose yourself."

Ravi asked, "Sir, what you told me is true? Have you faced similar situations in your life?"

"Yes Ravi! I have conquered the problems that came into my path. I have established a certain way to conquer problems and move ahead and that is why I am a Wealth Guru, remember that. I have guided many people and they are successful entrepreneurs now. They also have followed a certain way."

Ravi had somewhat calmed down. He asked, "Sir, will you please tell me how to overcome this situation? I will be more than grateful to you for that."

I said, "Sure, Ravi! That is why I am here. It is my mission and passion to help others. I will discuss with you some important topics that will really be helpful to you." I said in a soothing tone, "Now, regarding the situation you are in, I shall advice you to find one mentor who can guide you through it. You can ask him the way out or how to handle this matter. Now, take my advice, go home, take some rest and meet me tomorrow."

Ravi obeyed and left for home.

Chapter 4

Simple Pathway to Entrepreneurship

I had invited Ravi to my office the next day, as some of my wife's friends and their children were visiting our home. My office hours started early, because people used to come before their work began in the morning to take my advice as a Wealth Guru. Ravi came sharp at nine in the morning as usual. He was ushered inside my cabin by my receptionist. He asked my permission to enter and stood there with awe in his eyes, as he looked at the various certificates of excellence lining the wall. The medals and awards that I had won were arranged tastefully in a smart mahogany show-case situated opposite my table. Those things were symbols of some proud moments of my life. The huge table before me was entirely covered by a glass cloak, a personal computer, a laptop and two Parker pens arranged neatly in a crystal pen-holder which was a gift from one of my Japanese clients. Some photographs of celebrities visiting my office were arranged alongside the show-case that spoke of the range of clients I deal with! I looked into my Rolex wrist-watch and smiled at him and said, "You are very punctual, Ravi!" He had brought two bottles of hair oil with him to gift me. I welcomed him and beckoned him to sit in the heavy black leather chair across the table.

I greeted him with these words to his surprise, "Ravi, I want to do something that I could not do yesterday, as you were not in a mood to hear it. But, I will do it now!"

He was glaring at me, wondering what that might be… "I want to congratulate you on your failure, Ravi!" I exclaimed in a joyous voice. He was completely astonished to hear me. Probably, he was thinking that I had an attack of madness!

"Sir, are you joking or teasing me?" he asked, still not believing his ears.

"Ravi," I said, "I am serious! I really want to congratulate you, because, failure is the first step towards success. All successful people in this world have faced some kind of failure in their lives. Actually, failure is the TEACHER. You know, most of our learning happens when we fail. When you walk on the pathway to success, learning stops somewhere. When you are at the top, you tend to pay less attention to learning new things. We try to learn new things when nothing works for us. Or, I will put it in simple words. The valleys are always lush green and there is very less greenery at the peak of the mountains."

The astonishment on Ravi's face was fading now and he seemed assured that I was not talking to him sarcastically. I continued, "So, thank you Ravi for failing fast and I really congratulate you for failing within a year of your business. Failing fast is the first success 'Mantra' for any new startup. Most of the people take two or three years for their first failure. You would be surprised to know that there are consultants who help the startups to fail early."

"One of my friends is giving this kind of consultancy in the United States. She helps the startups in the Silicon Valley to fail early. It is commendable that you have failed in a very short period without any consultant." The astonishment on Ravi's face returned again, but this time it was accompanied by a smile! He was very much interested in what I was telling him.

He said, "Sir, this thought is totally new to me. Tell me more about it."

I was glad that I was able to capture his interest with much less efforts. I said, "I had told you that day, there is a simple pathway. And to start walking on it, you have to surrender before it. This has worked for me and I assure you that it will definitely work for you. It begins with one simple step and that step is 'thinking'. We human beings create new things first in our thoughts. We are given the magical gift of thinking by our Creator. We have this powerful tool called brain at our disposal and it works 24x7 for us. The brain has boundless abilities. The only drawback is that, we have not trained it enough to think in a certain way. Why is this process important? Because, when we think in a certain way, we visualize what we want. It helps us to focus on the things we want and keeps us away from the unwanted things. This thinking ability can be developed by sheer practice. As I told you earlier, we are not trained to think. You have to sit in silence and concentrate your mind for this process to begin. Then you ask yourself what you really want. This is the very first step. The second step is being ready with a pen and paper to write down your wishes. What are my goals? What are my wishes?"

Ravi was thinking now. I asked him, "So, what do you want in life? Which car? What kind of house? How many people working for you? Do you want to be a millionaire or a billionaire? Do you want your income in rupees or dollars? Do you want to see the whole world? Don't you want to be ultra-rich? Just prepare a wish-list of your own. That will give you an access to think over it... right? The list will make your dreams clear, for yourself, for your family and for the whole society."

"How much money do you want in the first, third or the fifth year? If you want to visit distant lands, it will give you the clarity about which countries you are going to visit in these five years. If you put your plans on paper, you will have a complete picture of what you really want to achieve. While writing down you will come to know about your particular wishes and passions. If you are able to connect your passions with your business, be it manufacturing, trading or even your Yoga classes or Ayurvedic therapy, you will then thrive in your business easily and gracefully.

I also want to suggest that, there should be support from your family and friends."

"Why is it important?" Ravi asked.

"Because," I said, "they are the most important people around us and they contribute greatly to our growth, to our existence. They bring a great difference in our lives. They also have some kind of expectations from you, as you are a part of their life. You can add those expectations to your wish-list, so that you can fulfill them. Secondly, it will help you in a great way to achieve your goals. Once you have decided upon your business, speak with your family and friends. Get them aligned to your idea. Many entrepreneurs make this mistake of not confiding in their near and dear ones and they feel lonely."

Ravi said, "I had never thought of this, Sir! Tell me more about it. How can I do this?"

"The solution is," I went along, "to create a home team. For that, you have to convince your family about your business plan and take them into your confidence. If you can convince them, you can convince anybody in this world!"

"There can be difficulties in convincing them all, as each one might have a different opinion," Ravi put forward his concern.

"Yes, you are right, Ravi. Some of them might say, you can't do this, you will suffer, and no one in our family has done this before, etc. etc. That is why it is important to have their consent and confidence. And for that, you must have patience and confidence in yourself and in your business plan.

What I am telling you has a major spiritual aspect too, Ravi," I said. "Each one of us is a source of energy. Actually, we are centers of energy. You are one center and each one in your family is an energy center. When you bring them together, all the energy centers will come together and by using the accumulated energy, you will speedily go ahead in your business and achieve your goals."

"Sir, please tell me step by step how I should start working now on," Ravi said eagerly.

I smiled. The worry and sorrow of failure that had left marks on his forehead were disappearing now. Here was a young man, full of dreams and ideas about his future. I told him, "First of all, make a wish-list and convince your family and friends. You now have to think in a certain way and this is what I call a certain way. Let me elaborate. You want to have a car, for example. You have written so in your wish-list. Writer Rhonda Byrne has written in her famous book 'The Secret' that whatever we get and do not get is because of the 'law of attraction'. So, for fulfilling your dream about a car, you should start visualizing it, and for doing this, you have to see a picture of the car or go to a show-room and take a test drive. Then you will have a clear image of the car in your mind. Then come home and sit in silence or go to any place of your choice, where you can think. Put this image of the car on the ultimate source, which is the Universe.

The Universe understands your language because we are a part of Nature and Nature knows how to create things for us. Just by visualizing and thinking, you will receive what you want, provided you act in a certain way. We will see now what that way is.

The very important aspect is to work on oneself, and right now, you have to bring a 360 degree shift in your looks, language and behavior, your thinking and acting.

Also, think about the company you spend your time with. Who are your friends? One proverb says that, 'Show me your friends and I will tell you who you are!' So, think about who you are rubbing your shoulders with. You slowly become those with whom you spend more time. I can imagine those people who are always with you. They influence you greatly and because of their company you attract poverty."

Ravi seemed surprised to hear this and murmured, "Ohh! This is what it is? Tell me more, Sir. I want to think about it."

"Yes Ravi," I continued, "Now as you say that you want to become rich, you have to be in connection with successful entrepreneurs. You should connect with certain groups of creative and inspiring people; it would add more value to your planning. The new generation of entrepreneurs really inspires me by their thinking and the way they act. Most of the time, we think that our ideas are not working and we try to find out more suitable circumstances to help them work. But, in fact, we have to work in two ways; on the business and on the businessman. Right now, we are working on the business person that is 'self'. The transformational shift in your self will bring the desired change.

Ravi, what you achieve in your business and your life begins with you. YOU are the source of that change. It will start with taking command of your life. You may have questions as how to actualize this. Taking your own responsibility begins with your willingness to take it. Are you willing to be your own master?" Ravi nodded in agreement. "This is your life and the reason of your failure in your first business is not the circumstances. It all happened because of you. You were responsible for that failure. Your principal commitment is to clear all that mess. How fast you clear that up will determine your future developments.

Firstly, it is about the entrepreneur and then it is about the entrepreneurship. And being an entrepreneur, there are various aspects of entrepreneurship. To become a successful entrepreneur, you should have a thorough knowledge of the domain of business."

"Sir, what you are telling is very interesting," Ravi said, "tell me more about business."

"Business is a very different phenomenon," I said, "We have a certain concept about business, but we are not clear about how to do a business. So, the ability to visualize how your business concepts will work practically at the time of implementation is the phenomenon. Developing this ability is the real game. For that, you have to gain a thorough knowledge of the business domain. Internet is the best source for doing this. It will make tons and tons of information available to you. You should have a complete knowledge about the business you want to do. But, the knowledge alone will not be enough. Implementation of that knowledge will make all the difference. The next aspect is learning the language of business.

You should always be on your guard and watch your word in business commitments because, 'your word is your world and your world is your word'. Our day to day language is different from the language of business. Various businesses have their own languages. If you are a doctor and you are in the Operation Theatre, you will not say, 'give me that knife', instead, you will say, 'scalpel'."

"Sir," Ravi asked, "where would I get all this knowledge?"

I said, "For that, you have to rub shoulders with those who are already in that business. You have to participate in seminars, gatherings, training programs, etc. You can gain the knowledge there and it will connect you with the cult of entrepreneurs as well. One simple connection can help you to fulfill your wish-list. This is the power of networking. You have to reach out to people, learn from them and listen to their experiences. Build upon what you know and just implement that knowledge. Whatever is useful for your business, take it and leave out that which is not useful. You might feel that some information is irrelevant for the time being, but it might turn out to be useful in the future, who knows? Nothing goes waste."

We had been talking for a long time. We both needed a break, especially Ravi. I called my office peon Hari, and asked him to bring coffee and sandwiches. Ravi must be hungry, I thought. He became somewhat awkward as he thought that he had taken up much of my time. But I assured him that it is my profession and passion, and listening and talking to people is routine for me. I offered him the sandwich. He thanked me and we had the much-needed break.

Refreshed after that intermission, I began, "What I was telling you, Ravi, is that everything counts in business, your failure too! It taught you how to settle a debt, how to manage finances, how to sell a product, what to do and what not to do in business, etc. If you want to be an entrepreneur, your first job is to learn to speak the language of business. Other than that, you have to be a good orator. If you are not, then it is fine. It is not that all the successful businessmen are good speakers, but to inspire your team to do the business, you should be able to communicate well with them. Effective communication is important. If you don't know this language, learn it. If you don't want to learn yourself, hire someone who will speak for you. As yours is a startup, I would advise you learn it yourself; it would be better and it is not as difficult as you might think.

New language and effective communication will make new contacts for you. People will come to you. I want you to be an inspiration for others. When you go and attend business meetings and conferences, people should think that – "I want to be like him." If you are able to generate this feeling in people, your job is half done."

Ravi asked, "My appearance will also count. What is your opinion, Sir?"

"Yes Ravi," I said, "appearance counts in business, the way you talk, the way you walk… I don't mean it is everything, but it definitely adds value to your personality. Everything counts in entrepreneurship."

"Sir, tell me more about how should I develop my personality?" Ravi asked. He was eager to know.

"You have to read books to get more knowledge; books related to your business, related to the idea that you intend to work upon. Read biographies, inspiring stories of successful entrepreneurs, who had started from scratch. For example, you would be surprised to know that Apple and Google took birth in a garage! AIRBNB was started in a 10x10 sq. ft. basement. Participating in workshops will also help you. This initial inspiration may not last long and you might lose it in future, so you have to make a systematic plan.

Make a plan for the next one or two years. That should include all the actions you intend to take. Many calendars are available online. Make use of them, they are free of cost. There must be one person who will hold you accountable for taking the effective actions that will produce the intended results, and when you fail or fall, you can go to that person. Find out one mentor for yourself, who will actually coach and guide you on day to day basis in doing business."

I had finished my talking; but Ravi still looked restless. He was obviously engrossed in the thought of his debts. I considered the situation for a moment and decided that until he pays his debts he would not be ready to take in the advice that I was giving to him. So, I said to him, "Ravi, I think that you should take a short break and go for a trip to some distant and serene place, probably to the Himachal. Calm yourself down and restore your mind's peace and then come to me."

Ravi nodded and said, "Thank you Sir for giving me this advice to take a break. I really need one. I will see how I can manage that, as I have no money left; but I have a strong desire to go to the Himachal. I will take your leave now and will call you after I return."

So, he left my office and I wished him good luck for clearing his debts.

Chapter 5

Blueprint of Business

Days went by. It was almost two months since Ravi had left my office on that day. One day while I was chalking out my new series of lectures to be delivered in the next week in Delhi, my intercom rang and the receptionist told me that a young man wanted to meet me. I permitted to let him in and Ravi stood at the door of my cabin. He looked very fresh, clean-shaven and with a twinkle in his eyes. This time he came with a parcel of bathing soaps and gave it to me. I thanked him and said, "Hello Ravi, you are looking good! Where were you all these days? Have you been to the Himachal?"

Ravi said, "Sir, my brain had stopped working after I took your leave. There were so many things to be sorted out and how I had messed up with my business, etc. I was lost in thought for two days. On the third or the fourth day, my businessman friend, Shubham, met me. He is a successful real estate business person. He asked me, "What are you doing nowadays Ravi?" I said, "Nothing… I am doomed at my business and bankrupt." After listening to my story he said, "I am going to Himachal with some of my friends. I love Himachal. Why don't you join us?" I had heard a lot about the natural beauty and the scenic spots of that place, as you also must have known Sir, but never had a chance to go there. But, alas! How could I? "I don't have money," I told Shubham.

He said, "Don't worry. Your company is enough for me. I will pay all your expenses. You pay me later when you get money.'"

"So, it was settled and I went with Shubham and his two friends. We went to Dalhousie, Chamba and Khajjiyar. Sir, those ten days changed the whole course of my life. First, we went to Dalhousie. Dalhousie is famous for its untouched natural beauty and peaceful environment. It is a very peaceful place. It was the rainy season, and you won't believe it, but you will find clouds with you in your living room! It is a small town with a mall road and a few shops. The roads are single lane; still not so narrow that only one vehicle would be able to pass. But, you have to be careful while driving. The atmosphere was so soothing that my wounded and restless mind found some peace. And I was with so different a company, all bachelors and successful businessmen, that I almost forgot about my failure.

Then we moved on to Khajjiyar. If you really like nature, then move towards Khajjiar and other nearby places. Khajjiar is a good place to spend a full day in the beautiful green grounds, surrounded by Devdar and Pine trees and hills. It is called mini Switzerland. We also visited an old Temple of Five Pandavs here. Other than this, you have the option to visit the wild life sanctuary (Kalatop) between Dalhousie and Khajjiar. However one local resident told us that you won't find many animals there. Still we enjoyed the nature and some adventure also.

While going to Khajjiar from Dalhousie, we had to go up towards the top of the hill from the junction of the wild life sanctuary. There we found very beautiful scenes and a number of places. We had some good camera shots."

Ravi was engrossed in his account of the tour. But, I did not interrupt him. He went on.

"Then we decided to go to Chamba valley. The valley is unique in its surroundings, which offers breathtaking views of the peaks. The nature has endowed Chamba valley with exotic beauty, which is reflected in its picturesque landscapes, surrounding greenery and rich wildlife. The spectacular beauty of the snow clad peaks leaves you spellbound throughout the journey. It is popularly known as the Ravi Valley. Small villages and hamlets extending over the landscape provided delightful sights."

"We then went to Dharamshala as I wanted to visit the Dalai Lama Ashram. Dharamshala is truly a very spiritual place; you must have known Sir, but still I want to tell you," Ravi said.

"Yes, yes, go on Ravi," I encouraged him.

He went on, "There are many Buddhist cultural and health and healing spots in Dharamsala. You can pray for peace at the Dalai Lama Monastery; that is the Ashram. You can feel the magical aura of the Holy Oracle of Dalai Lama and relax yourself with refreshing nature walks amongst green paddy fields and unexplored tea gardens in the quiet beauty of the hills. I found my inner peace there at the Ashram. I am glad that I took your advice and went there. It really helped me to heal my mind's scars. I feel that I am reborn now with refreshed vitality and ready to take life's challenges."

"I am very happy for you Ravi!" I said.

"Who were the other two friends?" I asked.

"They are also very successful businessmen like Shubham. During those ten days, they were continuously talking about their business and their new ventures. They told me that every year they take a break and go to some part of India for vacation. Sometimes they go out of the country and enjoy their free time."

Ravi was telling me, as if he was looking into his future!

He went on, "They also discussed what happened last year, what worked for them and what did not work in their business. They were sharing their plans for the next year. They all have very set formulas, Sir. While listening to them, I found my mentor in one of them. His name is Viraj Chaudhari. Sir, do you know Viraj?"

I smiled and said, "Yes. I do know him. He is a real estate giant and a very successful builder with innovative ideas. As a Wealth Guru, I come across many successful businessmen, but I have not met him in person yet though I would love to!"

Ravi nodded, "Sir, I requested him to be my mentor. I told him about you. He is highly impressed by your reputation and said, 'You are privileged and lucky that you had guidance from such a person.' He accepted my request. With the help of the tips you had given to me, I prepared a plan, a blueprint of my business, my vision, my mission… everything was ready on paper.

When we came back from our trip, I was so inspired and full of energy. Actually, I had not taken any action to fulfill my plan, but everything on paper looked great. I was pretty sure that I would achieve my goal because you were guiding me and now I had a mentor like Viraj Chaudhari and after spending ten days with this very inspiring company, I had started to believe in myself. I was confident that after executing my plans, I will achieve all my targets." Ravi said.

He was hesitating to speak further. I noted that and asked him, "Then what is the problem now?"

Ravi said, "Sir, before going any further, I wanted to take your advice. This is the reason I have come straight away to meet you. Should I take this plunge? Are there any dangers in it? Am I making the same mistakes as before? I want to clear all my doubts as I am going to do a business which is totally different from my first one. I have no experience in this real estate business and I want to take your guidance."

"Ravi, you are right there! You should not make haste. We will discuss this matter in detail. You should be all prepared for this new venture and then go ahead."

Ravi asked when I would have time for him to talk over this matter and I fixed an appointment with him for the next day.

As usual, he came sharp at nine in the morning and our talks began. "Ravi, today we will discuss about money. Yes Ravi, it is all about money, honey, it is all about money! Actually, getting rich is a very wonderful process and as a Wealth Guru, who will tell you this better than me? Sometimes, you might feel bored during that process, but money is an inspiration. Money gives you power, money adds value to your life and money gives you name and fame. It also gives you choices. And why are we discussing these things for hours? Because, "Jab tak aap ke paas paise hai, sab poochhenge aap kaise hai..." So it is said in Hindi. (All will greet you as long as you have money.) Money fulfills your wish-list and strengthens your relationships. It gives you access to the network of people who are richer than you. Money gives you happiness. It gives you the experience of abundance. So, you have to work on yourself and the business you are going to do to earn money, understand? Right now, we will look at what kind of business you are going to do."

Ravi nodded in agreement. I asked, "What kind of business do you want to do to begin with? Your business will make you ultra-rich and you had expressed your wish to be so. Doing a job also will help you in this, no doubt, but it is all about time. For example, for getting a good job you will have to give more exams, train yourself, get more education and then, one fine day, you might become a CEO of some company. This is one way of getting rich. But, looking at the current condition and situation of your life, I would suggest you to begin with a small business. You failed in your first business. There are many reasons, and one of them is that you started it on a large scale."

"In my opinion, to create something big and miraculous, you have to take a baby step. Actually, the journey of a thousand miles begins with the very first step. Why to do business? To fulfill your wish-list, isn't it? Otherwise, there is no need!"

"Basically, you don't need money to survive in this country. There are many resources available that would feed you without earning a single penny. There are so many NGOs, Ashrams, religious institutions, which give free food and shelter to the homeless and jobless. So, if you won't work, they will provide you food and shelter. As you see, survival is not a problem in this country. But, if you want to do something in life and become ultra-rich, business can give you everything faster."

Ravi asked, "What business would you suggest for me, Sir?"

"This is a wonderful question, Ravi! It depends on what business you want to do, because there are thousands of options available in this world. A few years back, nobody thought that certain things would be considered as 'Business'. As we see now, cell phone companies are in full bloom, television sets of unbelievable configurations are in demand. These products could not be imagined a few years ago. Even, selling water in bottles is very profitable business nowadays," I said.

"Very true, Sir," Ravi agreed, "It is unbelievable that water can be sold in this country, where giving water is considered a privilege."

I said, "Serving guests or any human being at the doorstep with water is the tradition of our country. These are our religious customs, as you know. Selling water is nowadays considered a religious deed! So, you can see that, anything and everything could be titled as 'businesses'. You can become a billionaire by selling even peanuts and chairs as well! Starting an online business can make you rich. Real estate business is a big domain under which you can sell plots, flats, buildings, nature homes and what not; that also will make you ultra-rich. Even selling plants, seeds and soil can make you rich! Writing and /or selling books can earn lots of money for you. There are thousands and thousands of ways of doing business. And there are thousands of businesses for you to choose from.

But what is the right business for you, that is the question you should ask," I said.

"That is exactly what I was thinking," Ravi said smilingly.

"It all depends upon your liking, Ravi and what you really want from your life, what really inspires you, what it is that you are passionate about," I glanced at him questioningly.

He replied without losing a fraction of a second, "I am passionate about serving people."

"That is great Ravi, but there are hundreds of ways of serving people, from washing their clothes to selling lands for them to invest their money. What exactly do you want to do? Think, what exactly inspires you. Then your passion will give you the answer!"

"Now, I am getting some light on this matter of business," said Ravi. "Please keep talking so that I would be clearer about my choice."

I continued, "Connect your passion to your business choice. Then you will come to the conclusion. Your decision should entirely be yours. It should neither be based on any suggestions or opinions of your family and friends.

You may get inspired by Microsoft and wish to start an IT business. Then, it is nothing but Bill Gates' inspiration. But, the important thing is what do you really want to do? That would be your own business, right? It should be something which touches your heart. If you can do this, you will succeed fast. Keep this in mind and act upon it.

Ravi, we are discussing about the business selection process. Internet is also a good tool. There are unlimited business ideas available on it. You can discuss this matter with your mentor. You can also meet successful entrepreneurs whom you know. They will throw more light upon this matter.

Ravi, mark my words, don't make haste. Hurry makes worry and this usually happens with the budding entrepreneurs, youngsters like you; they are good initiators but they are always in a hurry and want quick results. In fact, haste makes waste. Making money and becoming rich is a process which takes its own time. It depends upon the entrepreneur and the way he demonstrates the entrepreneurship. It depends actually on how you earn time, as time is really valuable."

"Sir, what went wrong in my first business? I want you to analyze my failure," Ravi said.

"Good question, Ravi. Let me tell you. What I gather from your account is this. In your first business, you just converted your idea into a business and started working upon it without proper thinking or writing it down on paper. You should first write down your thoughts that inspire you. Keep writing. Write down everything. Write down which business you are going to finalize. So, what is it? Is it the real estate? Then write down the bigger domain of real estate. Rate it on zero to ten scale. Think… what part, what type of business in real estate, because there are many aspects of this business. At the early stage, just write down the description of what you want to do and how you are going to do it."

"How can writing down help me Sir?" Ravi asked.

"Let me tell you. It really helps," I told him. "Write down who will help you, whom you will include in your team. Are you going to do it alone or in a partnership? Then write down the exact nature of what you want to create. What is the unique selling point (USP) of that product? First, make a blueprint. Don't go and act. The blueprint will give you clarity. Put everything on paper.

Make a diary for this purpose. You have to write down everything because business has many aspects. One of them is the product, and then comes the finances, then sales and marketing, the next is team and the last but not the least is leadership, which you are going to demonstrate. It is the vision and the mission of the business which you have to write down in the very beginning. It begins with the question – Why are you going to do this business? How are you going to do it? You have to answer the 5 Ws and 1 H…that is – Why, What, Where, When, Who and How."

Ravi's face was gleaming with enthusiasm. He exclaimed, "Sir, I am really impressed and inspired by what you are telling me. I am going to act upon it, as soon as I reach home."

"Be patient Ravi, don't make haste, I am telling you again and again! Initially, focus on only one business or on one aspect that you have chosen from the big domain. Focus on that. Don't diversify. Keep focusing, keep working. Once it is settled down as a core activity, then think about diversification for growth. Don't diversify for entertainment. Usually, business gives money and people get bored by doing the same work for years and so they diversify. Our job is to create a winning business plan. Any business plan has fundamental aspects. Other than that, small aspects should also be considered. Your blueprint is actually your future. Ask yourself and your financiers, how much money you are going to invest in the next five years. How much capital will you need at the initial stage?

Plan the finances. Take the help of your chartered accountant. You should hire someone who is ready to serve you at very little cost, of course. There are people who support budding entrepreneurs and startups, at very less cost, because it inspires them. If somebody is growing, he inspires other people. Prepare a business plan in such a way that all the relevant parties will earn money in that business. If you are the only earning member in your business and others are not, then your business will never prosper. After creating the blueprint, ask yourself this question – "Is this business going to fulfill my wish-list?", as you will be doing that business to fulfill your dreams, won't you? If it does not satisfy you, think again or rework on it. We Indians are very poor in our thinking; we hesitate to write down the figures of 100 million and 1000 million. It is all about money, honey and it is all about those zeros. So, I suggest you to do one exercise every day."

"And what is that, Sir?" Ravi asked.

"Tell five of your friends the figures or numbers in millions of which you are afraid. Start doing this. As you want to become ultra-rich, ask yourself, will this business make me ultra-rich? If the reply is 'yes', then finalize it; otherwise, rework on it. You can also study business models or blueprints made by other people. You can search on the net for this and you can also meet successful people. You can take the help of CAs, meet more and more people and share with them. At least, they will contribute to your business. Some of them may share and some of them may not. But, each human being wants to contribute to the success of others. Successful businessmen are contributors and that is one of the reasons of their success.

It is wonderful if your business is giving you money in rupees. But, if it is earning in dollars or in pounds or sterling, then it would be awesome! Don't you think so? Think of some way by which you can earn in dollars and other foreign currencies that will give you the power of leveraging. If you think from a domain of leverage, then your actions are automatically leveraged and we all love to take those actions that leverage us. But, first of all, thinking is the initial process and thinking in a certain way is itself thinking about that particular action which will leverage us. It will leverage the whole game. This will create more time for you and more money for you.

Ask yourself whether this business which you have planned now is future-proof."

"Sir, what do you mean by future-proof?" Ravi asked.

"I will clear my point by giving some examples. There were certain painters in the past, who used to print the flex for shops, etc., and they also painted good pictures of some of the film stars. They were in big demand at that time to draw on the shop-doors/ shutters. Then the digital technology came and they all vanished from the scenario and their art is history now. So, if you want to sell paintings by hiring some painters, you have to think about the future of this business. Is the digital technology still in demand? How to make it future-proof? I can give you many examples about these aspects later on. So, ask yourself, is my business future-proof? After all, we basically want to build a business for the next seven generations."

Ravi said, "I want to do business for myself, Sir. It inspires me."

"If that inspires you, do it!" I said. "But, doing a business for the next seven generations inspires me. That is why I always operate my business from that domain. And actually, I love to make my business seven generations-proof. Now, we will talk about funds, money, how to raise funds and why funds are necessary."

Chapter 6

Fund-Raising and Financial Management

We met on the next day again at my office. Ravi asked, "Sir, as we discussed yesterday, what if my business plan is ready, wish-list is ready, blueprint is ready and I have no money; then?"

I said, "I know that you don't have money. Actually, you have to pay back so much debt from your previous business…" I said softly. Ravi hung his head.

"Don't be ashamed Ravi. I know that you have to pay those debts and when it comes to money, people behave weirdly. I request you to be attentive, because the word money itself takes you to some different world. I have learnt this after dealing with so many people for so many years that, when it comes to money, some people stop speaking to you, some stop listening, people behave strangely, some exhibit nervous body language, they start doing things which are very irrelevant at that time."

"What you are saying is very true, Sir," Ravi said.

"The whole body language changes," I continued, "I don't know what these five alphabets MONEY have in them; but this word has immense power. People consider money as a power; it is a form of satisfaction for some of them.

It is domination and magic for some. Now, we are talking about how to raise money for your business. There are so many ways, but again, you have to think thoroughly before taking any action. Thinking about the money is the key, and right now, your reality is that you have to pay back people's money." Ravi nodded in agreement.

I continued, "Here we are talking about fund-raising. Thinking about fund-raising in the face of all the debts you have, is the power of thinking. For that, you have to build muscles. I am talking about the brain muscles and this can be done by practice. As you shared with me that you have been practicing the thinking exercise for the last so many days, I must tell you that here I am not talking about passive thinking. What is passive thinking? Passive thinking is when you sit back and thoughts come to your mind, thoughts come to your brain, your brain thinks automatically… that is called passive thinking. I am not talking about that. Right now, if I ask you to do an exercise about money for two minutes, which thought will come to your mind with priority? You will think about whom to pay first? What if I can't pay him for the next six months or so? What will he do? Will he shoot me? Will he put me in jail? Will he file cases against me? Your brain will think something like this, right?"

"Yes," Ravi said, "I am thinking about such things day and night. What else can I do, Sir?" He asked helplessly.

"Calm down Ravi!" I said, "I am not talking about passive thinking, rather I am talking about active thinking. In the face of all this reality, what do I want? I have this business plan, I have this wish-list, I have a family to feed, I want to see distant lands, I want to enjoy life and I want abundant money for that; I want to be ultra-rich and I want money for that. How to raise these funds? Ask your brain to think about that. Actually, it is the job of the brain. If you really want to experience abundance, if you really want happiness and satisfaction, learn to dominate and control your brain. Active thinking is one of the ways to dominate the brain."

Ravi asked, "How is it possible to dominate our own brain?"

"I don't mean domination in its literal meaning. Domination means actually asking your brain to work for you, which is your biggest asset," I said smiling.

"Yes, you have to give command to your brain to think about your business and raising funds. What is the first thought that comes to your mind? "I don't have money", right? Wonderful! That is good information. Then, what else? What can you do? There are various ways. Asking your brain to do active thinking is the first way. The second way is using the law of attraction. This law is the biggest tool which is again activated by the brain. Is it correct that, in your visualization, in your thoughts, you are constantly attracting money? If you read the book 'The Secret', it will help you in doing this exercise. It is really a wonderful book. Indians used this method 5000 plus years back. Our ancestors used this method in this country and that is why India was called 'Sone ki Chidiya', that is, 'a country having immense wealth'," I continued.

"Why was it called so, do you know? Because riches were the domain of this country and there were mostly rich people in this country. As the heirs of those ancestors, it is easy for us to create money. In the world of money, money and integrity go hand in hand." He nodded.

"Money is actually a promise. I f you look at those currency notes, there the promise from the governor is written like this, 'I promise to pay the bearer so much rupees or dollars'. In the world of money, what matters is this promise and those who honor their promise with integrity become rich faster. They get money; they get whatever amount they want. You have to develop your muscles of integrity and it is all about giving your word and honoring it. It is also about training your people to do the same and expecting this from others with whom you are going to do the deal or the people with whom you are dealing right now."

"Is there any easy way of fund-raising?" Ravi asked.

"There are hundreds of ways of attracting money. There are so many innovative ways. Again, for that, you have to do active thinking. What are these innovative ways? First is to go to people to whom you had not gone earlier for business, ask them for money and borrow from them. As far as possible, don't take money with interest. This is important. If you must pay interest, please ask them if they take the interest and they keep the principal amount for three years.

This is one way. The other way of raising funds is, selling certain stake of your business before beginning it, or when you are about to begin, and then sell certain stake to some passive investors.

You can do one more thing. Start a small business, make it big and sell the whole business. Selling some part of it is also an option. You can start your work and after reaching a certain level, go to a private equity player or a venture capitalist. At the very beginning, there are angel investors who put money on some good idea. They invest their money and their money works for them and they become rich faster. These are the various ways.

You can bring in an investor or a partner in your business. That is also one way of raising funds. There is one very wonderful way to raise funds. If you are going to create some products, sell them before the actual production. That is the western way of raising money. Selling the products before production with some incentives and using that money to manufacture that product, will keep your business lean. Keeping everything lean is the best approach initially. Some may call you frugal, let them; being frugal works initially. On the contrary, what do people do? What is their idea of doing business? Or, what did you do when you started your first business? You must have bought revolving chairs and air-conditioners and that glass cloak for the table and sofa-sets. Were all those things really necessary? Tell me Ravi.

Actually, commitment and your word are the most important factors regarding money in business and right now, you have to pay to so many people. I want to put some more light on this. People really don't want money. They want to see that their money is alive. If you can assure them in any way that their money is alive, many of them will support you. Some of them may give you more for your business. You have to think accordingly. As I told you earlier, you have a very good asset with you and that is your brain. Your brain is with you. You have to use it. It can create hundreds and thousands and millions of rupees.

I have faith in my formulas. They do work. Many people have followed them. I, myself, am also walking on this path. I can only assure you that the chances of your success are more than the chances of your failure." I assured him.

Then Ravi asked, "If I fail again, what next?"

"Fantastic, Ravi! Very good question!" I exclaimed, "If you fail again, attempt it for the third time. That is my advice. It is that simple. If you fail for the third time, attempt it for the fourth time. Attempt till you are alive and it works!

Once you have money and start your business, another very important aspect about money comes into the picture and that is financial management," I touched another topic.

"Yes Sir, this subject is very close to my heart, as I messed up my first business due to the lack of financial management," Ravi said.

We laughed and I started speaking.

"Most of the people get attached to money in such a manner that they become money, and money becomes them. They can't see other than that, any world outside of money. That's a very dangerous phenomenon. Such people drive their car on their own. They don't like to pay anybody.

"Being a millionaire or a billionaire and living life so frugally is a crime. As you get attached to the money, money runs away from you. That's what my mother always used to tell me. I'm not saying that you shall not think about money, but getting attached to it will not resolve the issue."

"Very true Sir!" Ravi agreed.

"As you get attached to money, the whole world shifts. Attachment and commitment are two different domains. You should be committed to money for creating the asset value, which you have defined to fulfill all your goals, and this stands to make you rich for the next seven generations. You should be committed for that and then you will find yourself free from the attachment of funds. It's like becoming *sthitpradnya* about money. Many of the entrepreneurs go through this process and those who become really *sthitpradnya* about money get more money. Money follows them, and this is the true leadership while demonstrating entrepreneurship on the court. This is what I think."

"This is altogether a new thought!" Ravi exclaimed.

"Why is financial management necessary? Why is it required? Tell me Ravi, why is it required?" I asked.

"Because, from what you have told me, I see myself making millions of money. The question is, what should I do with it?" Ravi asked.

"Exactly! Our clear context is to be rich, not only rich, but ultra-rich for the next seven generations. For this, you will have to manage the money. Yeah, the money management is the key and it has various aspects. It has various aspects of management. Financial management is not only about managing the cash you are receiving. It is also about the cash going outside of the organization. It is also about managing the assets. There are so many aspects and the first one is 'thinking and acting in a certain way.'" I said.

"I have seen that without reaching the real richness people start celebrations. They dance; start all gratification there for themselves and for their team members, but standing at the peak without reaching there is like being a billionaire in a dream. You should actually have billions of dollars with you. Your bank statements, your asset values should speak about that." I said and Ravi agreed to that.

"Ravi, it is possible to think like a billionaire. It is thinking about abundance. It is name and fame. It is all about making difference. It is about serving the society. Actually it is a life of a wealthy person. I call this thinking in a certain way."

"We will now discuss about financial literacy," I said.

"And what is that?" Ravi asked.

"That is what I am going to tell you. If you don't understand accounts I am okay with that, but you must understand the language of money. You must understand the language of billionaires. You must learn to access that circle of the billionaires. There is a certain way of going there and reaching there. One of them is financial literacy. Financial literacy begins with understanding money. Understanding how money is getting generated. What are the various sources of generating money? There is money in everything. Being an entrepreneur you have to train yourself in seeing money in anything."

"When you train yourself in such a way that you can see money in anything and everything, you become financially literate. How to do that? There are so many books available in the market. There are so many courses available like 'E3', like Robert Kiyosaki's series of books. By reading such books and doing such courses, you can elevate your financial literacy." I concluded the point.

"What is next, Sir?" Ravi asked. He was much absorbed in my talks and I was satisfied to see his eagerness.

"You should ask yourself, "How much money shall I earn? How much will my next seven generations require?" Understanding that, jotting down and creating that much money, this is called creating a goldmine! Along with that much assets, training the next generation in financial literacy as well as training the next generation to train the next generation in financial literacy is the key to getting rich for the next seven generations. But for that you will have to prepare your wish-list, gold list and dream list, what do you want in your lifetime what do you really want? Do you want a bungalow? Do you want a business setup in Paris? Do you want a business setup in Amsterdam or London or India? How much do you want for yourself, for your business; jot down everything. Make the total of all those expenses needed.

You should train your next generation for the same thing for the next generation. This will set you free. How much goldmine do I need? This is all about what I am talking about jotting it down; writing down how much gold I want from this goldmine. Taking all gold from that goldmine and keeping it safe and secure by using the financial literacy is important. Then it will grow day by day, moment by moment and generations by generations.

The next aspect is 'profit and cash flow'," I continued.

"An entrepreneur's principal commitment is to generate huge profit, and to manage the cash flow. These are the two principal commitments. But for that, you must understand the difference between cash flow and profit. Most of the organizations mingle these two things. Cash flow is money coming in and money going out, and managing that is called cash flow management. Profit is what you have gained after all the expenses; after products and cost, sales cost, after paying taxes. You can get better understanding of profit and cash flow from your charted accountants."

Ravi was listening keenly.

"As an entrepreneur your job is to build your asset column. According to me, minding your own business is minding your own asset column; and how to mind your own asset column? After looking at all your wish board, dream list, your requirements for next seven generations, you should generate that much asset column, which would fulfill all those needs. Each of your assets must generate income for you. Focusing on asset column without focusing on income column will resolve all your issues, as those assets will generate income for you and ultimately your entire asset column will grow. This is simply minding your own business.

If you try to do something other than this, you will put yourself in trouble, your organization in trouble, and your seven generations in trouble. Minding your own business by minding your own asset column is the key to all this. Actually what happens if you don't do this, I will tell you now.

When money comes, people forget their priorities. When money comes people start celebrating, they start producing some movies, they start social work, and some of them buy expensive cars or choppers, private jets, yachts, or immediately some expensive stuff, which doesn't generate any money."

"Sir, I did the same mistake while doing my first business." Ravi said with a shy smile on his face.

I nodded in agreement and said, "People say, "Yes, I am at the top now, I am everything, I understand each and everything, and nobody can teach me now, and that's it. I'm done." That's why within the next few years, they lose everything. They lose the money; their hard-earned money only by doing these things. They want to celebrate early. They want to give themselves and their team members so early, and that puts themselves and the organization in trouble.

There is another very important and interesting aspect," I said.

"What is it?" Ravi asked.

"That is, making an 'exit plan,'" I answered. "Exit plan is planning about our retirement and thinking if you really want to work further, for how many years do you really want to work with full enthusiasm, full of fun and drive? Are you passionate about your work; till what time will you love doing this? Plan that now. There are some business houses in this country which have handed over all their business to professionals and not their family members."

Remember one thing," I said. "While taking the exit, make sure that you have developed this from scratch. Make sure that it goes into the best hands, who will really take care of the next upcoming generation, as well as you did, and you will not have to look back again to take care of the organization or to take care of the business. That's the best exit plan according to me. Suppose you have ten years to retire, you can plan accordingly; you have time. Create more and more pipelines for your business, which will continuously pour money inside, so that you won't have to worry at all. Sometimes, if your followers do certain mistakes, the business can survive."

"Thank you Sir, for the valuable information! I did not know that there are so many aspects while starting a business," Ravi said.

We both needed a break, so we decided to meet the next day. I bid good bye to him. Off went that young man…with lighter steps, full of confidence.

Chapter 7

Sale Sale Sale!

Ravi came at nine in the morning as usual. This time he brought two bottles of Neem and Tulsi shampoo for me. He always made it a point to bring some Ayurvedic product with him whenever we met. I thanked him for the gift and said, "Shall we start Ravi?" He nodded.

"We talked about making a blueprint and fund-raising earlier, right" I started. "But one of the very important aspects is sales or selling your product. A sale is one of the key aspects of any business. It has direct linkage with the cash flow statement, with the profit and with the loan of the company. These are all linked to sales. If the sale of any of your companies is working, according to me, most of the things will work automatically on their own with very simple or very little efforts. According to my knowledge, 80 percent of the sales comes from 20 percent of the customers and 20 percent of the sales comes from 80 percent of the customers. So you'll have to find that out, where to focus your 80 percent sales, which usually comes from those 20 percent, so you'll have to decide how to take certain leverage actions in maximizing the sales. As you maximize the sales, automatically the turnover grows. As the turnover grows, profit grows and that's the cycle. You are in that positive cycle."

"But, how to increase your sales?" Ravi asked.

"That is what I will be telling here. As an entrepreneur, to build a business for the next seven generations, you have to be very opportunistic. How to see the opportunity? I will tell you a story about a shoe manufacturing company. They sent two sales persons to an African country and they asked them to make a survey there. One of the sales persons reported to the company that there was a big issue; nobody there was wearing shoes or chappals. He said, 'Please stop the production. We have to really work hard here to do the sales.' That's what the first one said. The second one reported to the company. 'Here is a tremendous opportunity. Only 5 percent of the people are wearing shoes or chappals, so please increase the production so that we'll sell more here and we will have huge profits as well as we will serve more customers.'"

"Ha Ha! What a drastic contrast!" Ravi laughed heartily.

"Yes Ravi," I said. "Looking at the same thing through a different perspective is one of the key abilities of an entrepreneur. Sales is actually you're selling the product and receiving the money which will be deposited in your account or in your company's account. Marketing is a systemized approach of creating awareness and allowing people, bringing people to the choice of whether to purchase that product or not. That's what marketing is according to me."

"Sir, you are putting everything in such simple terms that anybody can understand. You are truly a Wealth Guru," Ravi said.

I accepted his praise with a smile and continued.

"Sales can come from anywhere, there will be well-wishers. Well-wishers will be the source of branding. The best publicity in the world according to me is word-of-mouth publicity. All these people continuously talk about your product, and they are not asking you money for that. Most of the companies make quality products. But why only a few are successful is because they have different approaches of selling it. If you look at iPhone – iPhone's strategy is very different and I love it the most. They create hype of any of their products earlier and their products are so unique and they position it at a very high cost. Every time they come up with a very innovative product, they sell it at a very higher premium, that's their marketing and brand, and it's an established brand." I said.

"Sir, I have read about this. It is really astonishing. I wish I could create something like that…" Ravi mused.

"There are some really good books. I have read one titled 'How to sell anything to anybody', written by Joe Girard. Such books can also help you in this." I suggested.

Ravi noted this in his diary.

"As I was talking about the Apple product, when you look at any product, do you think that it's very challenging to make any quality product? Anybody can make it. But what's the difference between your product and your competitor's product? Ask yourself before planning any product or before launching any new product, 'What's the difference?' And nowadays, there are so much online data available. People can compare all your products with other available products." I continued.

"A lot of R & D will help in this. Data analysis and research and development will help you. For that, you will have to be an entrepreneur, you will have to search and find out what the real problem of society is or what people are facing. If you design a product which will be a clear answer or the solution to their problem, they will jump at any of your products. That's the way you will have to design the product. You will have to do certain market research and you have to keenly listen to what people are asking for, what's the issue they are really facing right now. You have to observe continuously."

Ravi nodded.

"Sir, I have seen many people selling their products at very low cost. Is it advisable? Can this help in increasing the sell?" Ravi was curious to know.

"Many times, people downgrade their prices to compete with the competitors. I think that's not the solution. Sometimes it may work. But if you are giving to people more in terms of values than the cash you are taking from them, they will jump for your product. That's the best pricing strategy for any other product. Whatever maybe your product… It may be real estate, it may be a car, it may be a cell phone or any online service business. So if you are giving people more in the values than the cash you are taking from them, they will jump for your product. That's the bottom line. Ask yourself, 'Which product will survive for the next seven generations and which will make them ultra-rich?' Will your existing product do this? You'll have to begin it from whatever infrastructure or whatever products you are having right now. You will have to build on it." I said.

"I agree with you Sir. What is the next principle? I am really interested in all this!" Ravi was excited.

"Place is the next important aspect," I said.

"See, these are the four P's of marketing which I'm discussing with you right now; product, price, place and people. The business schools are teaching this, so many books are talking about it, and when any conversation regarding the four P's comes, most of the business people say, oh I know this and what's new in this. I'm not talking about all that. Here I'm talking to you from a very different perspective. You have to dig down there. You have to dig down there really from your own context, from the context of your own business. If you dig it down there, something new will come up for you, right? If you really want to be successful, ask yourself, 'Is this the right place?'

Place is for where you are doing the business. Second is the place where you are staying. And third is the place where your product is getting used. You are doing business right now in a country like India where people speak so many languages and there are so many religions. And here you are doing business near Mumbai in Maharashtra and planning to expand all over the country and beyond, right? At how many places are you planning to go? What is the need of each place? Usually considering India, the need of Gujarat is very different from the need of Karnataka. The product you want to get sold in Kerala may not get sold in Himachal Pradesh.

So, place is a very important aspect. And also this is from the Indian domain. To be a business of the size you are talking about, you'll have to go globally and understand the culture of that place, understand what that community is facing, which is the biggest issue right now for them. After understanding that, sensing that, your team may give you the feedback, but actually as a business owner you have to take the ultimate call or you have to hire someone who will make that call for you. Getting that call and then bringing something for them and selling, is the real key. A certain place has so many aspects like culture, the age groups, and the climatic conditions. You have to take into consideration all these aspects.

As I said earlier, business means people, people and people! If you want to give them what they want, you will succeed. You will have to ask them and you will have to ask yourself what you really want. You need people to buy your products. You need people to sell your products and you need people to produce your products. It is all about people. So, sensing their problems and giving them the solution, you have to ask people what they think about your products on their own. The next level is, they speak on their own, without getting your encouragement. And for this, what works is the networking. The first circle in networking is your immediate contacts – your family, friends, neighbors, colleagues, extended family, people living in your building or colony, etc. Every person has at least 256 contacts. If you are able to use all those contacts, very soon you can reach in the global market. And when you get one contact in the United States, you automatically get 256 there. And when you go in any country in Africa, you get 256 and you get one contact, you get 256 contacts of that person." I told him.

"Really Sir! I never thought about this aspect," Ravi said enthusiastically.

"That's the simple logic of networking. And according to me, networking is not only connecting people. Networking is connecting the connections of that person, that's networking." I continued.

"The last but not the least very important aspect is innovative ways; innovative ways of sales and marketing. Right now the mantra of the market is go online; go online, everybody's doing that. Everybody's going online. Then let's do it. This is not an innovative way anymore but we can say, this is a new way, right? There was a time when I was struggling with my sales and when we were talking from the future sales perspective of the company, we were having one brain storming session. My mentor told me, "Have you ever thought about tapping all those students who right now are doing their graduation?" I said, "No Sir." And he said, "They are your future prospects."

"Right now you have to put at least 5 percent of your marketing energy here. They are your future prospects. There are so many other innovative ways and so many companies are doing it in different ways." I said.

"Ravi, do you know, why we are discussing all these aspects? All this is only for our customers. Customer is the king of this kingdom. He's king of his kingdom or queen of her kingdom. Why? Because he's someone who pays you. Some people succeed and some don't, only because they deviate from the needs of the customers and they fail," I said.

"Very true, Sir!" Ravi agreed.

"The best customer services according to me are keeping all your five senses open, and getting the sense of the customer. Customer is communicating to you through various ways. In fact that's why you're to keep your five senses open. Customer is your best teacher, customer is your best mentor, and customer is your best advertiser. He can become your best brand ambassador. You have to keenly listen to the customer, what he is saying. If you're offering your customer any of the products, and your customer says, 'Why is this function not in this item?' Or, 'I need this also.' Or, 'This is my requirement', you have to listen carefully.

If you're ready to take all these feed backs positively and are actually making certain changes, you'll be the king of the market because it's all about customer, customer and customer! Listen to your customers keenly, deliver what's needed; you'll be the king of the world.

I will share one of my experiences with you here. When I visited Macau, I saw how an entrepreneur can increase his sell through establishing a certain system, after putting an innovative idea into reality." I said.

"I am very much interested to hear it," Ravi said.

I began, "A few years back, I was visiting Macau for the first time. I was staying in a big hotel. At the ground floor of that hotel, there was a casino. Most of you know that Macau is very famous for these casinos and gambling games. I don't remember exactly the number, but there were 700 to1000 tables or those slotting machines or those game machines. Minimum four people were there at each table, on some four to ten, twelve, and twenty. All of them they were taking out their credit cards, buying those tokens, and playing with all those tokens.

I was just taken over by that entire ambience. There were money exchange counters at various places in that very big hall. So many arrangements were there. When I started looking at and calculating the whole game, I saw there were people from around the world. Each one of them was either giving cash or using their credit cards and they were continuously swiping those credit cards. Every deal was going on and people were paying. There was no owner there. Most of the people were not even aware who is owner of this property, but continuously 24 × 7, people were swiping their cards there. Continuously, they were putting some cash on those counters. I expect creating something like this. I am not talking about the gambling business; please note that… But I am talking about creating certain system which will inspire people to swipe their cards globally 24 × 7 × 365. Creating such a thing is the key for getting rich for the next seven generations; getting ultra-rich for the next seven generations. If you are sleeping and you are not making money, you will never be rich!

And above all, keep this in mind that you have started a business to facilitate your own needs. You should make it profitable. Then only you can survive in this vast business community. And for that you have to promote your product shamelessly, barefacedly and unblushingly!" I concluded.

Ravi rose to his feet. He was beaming with confidence. His eyes gleamed with satisfaction. He said, "Sir, thank you so much for giving me your valuable time! I will go now and try to implement your advice and I will meet you when I become ultra-rich."

"Okay Ravi. Let us hope that this works and you will be out of your debts as early as possible. I wish you good luck!" I said. "But remember that after clearing your debts, come to me and we will discuss further aspects of entrepreneurship. Do not make haste to start a new venture. I want you to start your new business after you are fully prepared for it," I cautioned him.

He nodded hastily and went away… I was not sure if he took my suggestion seriously.

Chapter 8

Yes... I Am Rich Now...!

Time went by. Almost three years passed and there was no news of Ravi. Sometimes I would wonder what he was doing, but slowly his name faded away from my memory. I was busy with my other clients as a Wealth Guru and my other businesses.

It was a Tuesday. I was staying at my farm-house for a while, as I wanted a break from the daily grind of city life. My farm-house was not so far from the city, but situated in a tranquil area. It was truly a farm-house with two hundred mango trees, a grape vine and a big farm for growing vegetables. When I came out of the house in the morning I looked at the property in satisfaction. It was a beautiful three-storey structure, very tastefully decorated with a swimming-pool, a spa and a well-equipped gym in it. I was taking my usual morning walk at 6.30 and my cell phone rang. I wondered who it might be at so early an hour... I saw Ravi's name flashing on the screen. I was surprised to see it and wondered what made him call me after one year!

I picked up the phone. Ravi said, "Sir, I want to meet you, very urgent, very important..."

I said, "Ravi, you are calling me after three years and at a very odd hour. And you are saying that you want to meet me urgently. Are you out of your mind? I don't know how to deal with you…but it's okay…what happened? What is so urgent Ravi?" I was somewhat irritated.

Ravi said, "Yes Sir, this is one of those situations of life and death for me and it is a great mess. I don't know how to handle it," his voice cracked with emotions.

I had calmed down a bit and sensed that there must be something serious. "Is everything alright, Ravi?" I asked.

"Yes," he said, "all other things are alright, but one thing has happened and the situation has become disastrous. This has nothing to do with my business, but… Actually Sir, I don't want to talk over the phone. Rather I want to meet you immediately."

So, it was serious…! I said to him, "Okay Ravi. Come over here at my farm-house. It is a ten minutes' drive from your home. Come at around 8.30, we will have breakfast together." I put the phone down and went inside to freshen up.

He came sharp at 8.30. As I looked at Ravi, I saw that his face was aghast and very pale and unshaven for at least two to three days. He had not even combed his hair. It was apparent from his eyes and overall appearance that he had not slept for two to three nights. I asked, "Ravi, what happened? You look totally shattered. You look as if you have not slept for hours."

"Hours!" he exclaimed. "Sir, I am awake since three days and nights!"

"Oh! Then it must be a very disturbing matter. What happened?" There was concern in my voice now.

"There is a big fight between me and my fiancée," he said.

"Your fiancée? When did you get engaged?" I was astonished.

Now, he seemed to realize that we had not communicated with each other for the last three years! A sheepish smile appeared at the corners of his lips and he said in a tone of apology, "Sorry Sir! I will explain everything. First of all, let me apologize to you for not communicating for so many days. But, whenever there is any problem in life, I remember only you Sir! I think that you can deal with that situation; I admire you most and love you. You are my power-house! I will begin from where I left you one year back."

"Okay, good! Have a seat and relax yourself," I said. Leaning back in my chair and looking into his eyes, I said, "Yes Ravi, I still remember you had said, 'I will become ultra-rich and then I will meet you.'"

"Yes Sir, but I have already done that. I will not claim that I have become ultra-rich, but I am rich enough to manage myself, my wife-to-be, my kids-to-be and my entire family. That much money I have earned. I am meeting you today in an emergency situation."

The Wealth Guru in me was pleased to hear his progress. "Fantastic! I am proud of you Ravi!" I appreciated him.

"So, what happened now?" I asked.

"Do you remember the last time we met in your office?" he asked.

I nodded.

"Then I left you and went home." Ravi continued, "I was thinking for two to three days, how to begin. I did not know at that time how to pay the debt that amounted to almost sixty-five lacs to all my creditors. You know all about that mess."

"Yes, yes, I know that," I remembered the whole account of his first failed business.

"What did you do after we discussed the three principles – blueprint, fund-raising and sale, sale, sale?" I asked.

"As you know that I met my mentor Viraj on that Himachal trip. I had come to take your advice after the trip. I took your leave and met Viraj. We finalized my plan as per the strategy. Viraj asked what I was going to do about money, as I did not have any. Then I asked Shubham if he could give me some money to start with," Ravi told me. "Actually, my plan was to take some property for sale, as I had told you in our last meeting I wanted to start a real estate business. Shubham is a very successful builder and a very good friend of mine, as I have told you. I asked him, 'Well, why don't you give me five flats of your building that I will sell in the market? You take your rate and I will take my profit.' Shubham said, 'See Ravi, though we are friends, business is business. Don't mingle it with friendship. If you need any help in the future, I will be there to help you, but at present, you find some money on your own.'"

"He did a right thing, didn't he?" I asked.

"Yes Sir. I couldn't blame him. Nobody wants to put money on the losing horse!" Ravi said smilingly. "My plan was to take some units in a building or in a layout of plots and make bulk bookings. And give those bulk bookings to the owner of that business. After coming from the Himachal, I went from door-to-door of various offices of real estate players in my town. Nobody entertained me and most of them made fun of me. Some said, 'Why don't you give me some money first? I can't give you my property for selling without you giving me money.'" Ravi said.

"And the creditors; what did you do about them?" I asked.

"What could I do? I found myself in the same situation again with the creditors at my back. You know that they followed me on telephone to the Himachal also! They started demanding their money after I returned. The person from whom I had taken loan at five per cent interest was threatening to shoot me. I lived under the fear of death. Nothing was working." He said.

"Yes, I remember Ravi. You had told me this in our last meeting," I said.

Ravi continued his story, "One fine evening, I was strolling aimlessly on College road. A motorbike stopped near me. I was delighted to see my old friend from college days. He said, 'Hey Ravi! What a pleasant surprise! What are you doing here?' We hugged each other. I told him that I was just roaming as I had nothing to do. We went to a 'chai katta' and I told him everything while we had a cup of tea."

"He listened to me and then said, 'There is one company that can help you in doing this. Why don't you go and meet them?' I said that I did not even know them. He said, 'Come with me. I am also working with them.' He took me to that office. That company was Wealth Zone. He directly introduced me to the sales director of that company. I will make it very short. I entered there in this fashion." Ravi said.

I was eager to know what happened next and asked him so.

Ravi told me, "The director asked, 'What do you want?' I said, 'Sir, I want to repay 65 lac rupees of debt.' He stared at me in disbelief. 'I can't give you money!' he said. 'I don't want money from you Sir,' I told him. 'But I want your support in generating money and I want to create a win-win situation for both of us. I am not asking you any favors; instead I want a discount from you. I have met eighteen people in this last three to four days. Nobody listened to me. I want your support and some discount. I want to earn one crore rupees in one year.' He was staring at me as if I had fled there from an asylum! He let me stand there and talk only because of my friend who took me there with him. Thanks to him the director showed at least some interest in me. Sir, why was I able to do this, do you know?" Ravi asked.

"Because, I had prepared a blueprint and while working together, Viraj and I had decided on this magical figure. As I had to pay 65 lacs with interest, it amounted to 75 lacs. So, I would earn around 25 lacs that year. Everything would turn around. We had studied that much.

So then, the director asked, 'Fine! What do you want? We are in the business of selling plots – non-agricultural plots around Mumbai, in the outskirts of Mumbai. If you sell them for us, you will get a good commission. We pay good commission to our business associates.' I said, 'I want something more.'"

"Good Ravi, I like your confidence!" I said. "What did you tell him?"

"Before I said anything, he asked, 'Why don't you go for a bundle of bread, if you want something more? Will you be able to sell?' I said, 'Yes, selling is my passion. I can sell anything to anybody and at any place.' He was very pleased to hear my answer and said, 'Wonderful! Then I am with you.'"

The Wealth Guru in me was also pleased to hear Ravi's story. He was following my advice and generating money. My interest rose regarding the further developments in Ravi's life. I beckoned him to continue.

"The director said a single sentence then, 'Don't worry, I also have gone through such situations in my life. Life throws anything towards us. As an entrepreneur, we can succeed if we can take those challenges.' I asked him how he could help me. He said, 'If you buy some plots in bulk from me, I will give you a good discount. If you buy twenty to fifty plots, then the discount is more. But, you have to sell the plots in one year.' I agreed and paid Rs.1001/- as a token of that deal."

"I replied, 'Okay, I can easily do that.' He asked me again, 'Are you sure, will you do that in one year?' I assured him that I could sell in ten months. He gave me all the promotional material, brochures, layout, etc. Then he marked the blocks and all the interiors. We shook hands. The deal was done."

I also wanted to shake hands with my daring disciple and did so.

Ravi went on with his story, "The moment after coming out of his office, I went to one of my uncles and said, 'Uncle, you know that my bad time is going on and I want money. What will you say to this?' Uncle was very skeptical, he said, 'I don't give money to those who don't know how to handle it. You are already in a huge debt, how can you start a new business? Are you out of your senses?' I ignored his sarcastic remark. I remembered what you had told me, 'you have to promote your product shamelessly, barefacedly and unblushingly'. I said stubbornly, 'But I don't need your money. On the contrary, I have brought a good investment opportunity for you. Your money will be doubled in two or three years. It is a very good location.' Still he refused to consider my proposal. He asked me to show my ability by doing one of his incomplete tasks. It was regarding his pension. He was not getting it for some reason. I asked him about his office and the office name reminded me that one of my friends had some kind of connection with that office. I went to him and asked for his help. My friend had a friend of his in that office and he agreed to look into that matter and he kept his word. Some technicalities needed to be completed and he did that. My uncle started receiving his pension! He was happy to see my efforts and finally was ready to listen to my proposal. He agreed to visit the plot, liked it very much and I did my first sale."

He continued, "I did not think at that time, what would happen if that director refused to pay me as all the plots were in his possession. He could have shunned me away, Sir, as there was no written agreement between us. But, I remembered your words that business happens in commitment. One's word is most important in business. I believed in you, in that man, in myself and here I am now, standing before you as a successful businessman. It was just a gentleman's promise and he honored his word and I also did my best. Within the next four months, I sold almost all the plots! The first thing I did was to pay the man from whom I had taken money at five per cent interest. This is how my first attempt of generating one crore rupees got completed. I earned around 35 to 40 lac rupees from this deal." Ravi said with pride. His achievement was commendable indeed!

I asked him, "Ravi, tell me in detail how you went about the whole business."

"Sir, I still remember everything. I will tell you. It was the first day of Diwali and I was at home. It was the first week after I had started selling plots. Otherwise, for the last so many months, everybody at home was telling me that, 'Do a job again, this is not your cup of tea. Nobody in our family has done any kind of business. There has not been a single businessman in our family for the last seven generations,' etc, etc." Ravi said.

I smiled, "I had told you this exactly in the same words one year ago, hadn't I?"

"Yes Sir, you said it right! My parents were saying that we would sell our house and shift to a rented home and pay all the debts. But, I was very happy on that Diwali day, because I had sold one plot to that stubborn uncle of mine. I told this to my father. He said that if I could sell to him, then I could sell anything to anybody. And his words of encouragement inspired me. That is how my first baby step, as you named it, was successful. After that, the sales director and the other directors became my friends. With the completion of this deal, they felt that Ravi delivers what he says.

The director and I met once again, but this time not in his office. We had our meeting at a well-known resort near our town in the 'green valley'. We had a great party to celebrate our success and during the party, he again asked me, 'What do you want from me?' And I said, 'I want two crores in the remaining eight months.' This time he agreed without asking any question. He seemed more enthusiastic than before and eager to deal with me, because as you had said Sir, everybody likes the person who delivers! Everybody believes in the person who gives results. He showed more confidence in me as his sales partner. He gave me a bunch of plots at bulk rate. And Sir, you won't believe, I sold all of them in seven months!"

"How did you do that?" I asked.

"Sir, I planned a strategy based on the three aspects of entrepreneurship you had shared with me. I remembered that you had asked me to think in a certain way and realized that I was thinking in a certain way! Someone better off in business had told me to do so – imaging and visualizing how it would look like on court. I came to know then the difference between a concept and phenomenon. Earlier, I used to listen to this as a concept; but now I am doing this as a phenomenon. I can correct my mistakes in my thoughts and visualization. All this was good; but as I was not the master of the law of attraction I could not sell enough plots as per my own expectation.

People refused to listen to me. I was again depressed. But I remembered your words, 'an Entrepreneur never gives up!' So, I thought I would try my best. I started to go to various conferences and seminars. Once I went to a conference organized by the 'Dalit Entrepreneur Cell of India – DECI'. I met many influential people there. I met Sunil Kamble there. We talked and he listened to my story. He invited me to his office in Mumbai. I went to Mumbai the next week. We shared our experiences. Sunil said that he also had gone through bad days; he also had committed mistakes like me. He said that he is much impressed to see me applying a very systematic approach in business now. He introduced me to some of his acquaintances. He gave me leads to approach the people of our community who were very well off in life.

Two or three people listened keenly to me and decided to buy plots." Ravi said.

"That is good Ravi, I am much impressed!" I said.

He continued, "Sunil and I decide to arrange a get-together of our community. People came there and they were impressed by my way of talking, thinking and authenticity. I gave them a handsome group discount and my first bulk sell happened there. Then one day, I met one friend of mine at a cinema. He invited me to his home. I went and he introduced me to his father, who is a CEO of an established company. He was glad to listen to me and asked me to meet the investors related to his company. I met those interested people and they agreed to invest in plots. This way, I made my second bulk sell. My network expanded as they introduced me to their network. They started believing in me. This happened due to your teachings Sir!"

I said with a twinkle in my eye, "Yes, I do believe you Ravi, I DID believe you. I am Wealth Guru and I know where to invest my valuable time! I believed that you would deliver for sure. I had noticed that spark in you. Okay, what did you do next?"

"I repaid all my debts, as I got ample amount in this deal. My father was very much worried about the education of my siblings, so I gave some money to him and that gave me immense happiness. And from that day, I have never looked back."

"Tell me more, Ravi," I said eagerly.

"The Wealth Zone company people took me as their project partner. They said, 'Don't give us a single penny, you just sell. And you will get your percentage.' So, today, I am doing my own business as well as I sell for them because nobody has given me such opportunity. I exist because of them. I learned business strategy from them."

"Oh! So, you have started your own business?" I asked, a little surprised...

"Yes. The chairman of that company and the sales director supported me. One day they said, 'Why don't you start your own business?' I told them that construction is my liking. I wanted to construct big buildings, skyscrapers. They said, 'Good! We are not in this business, but you can do it.' They offered me their lands. They wanted some share in the constructed property. That is how it all started and now I do 80% of my construction on their sites. This way, I need little capital. Whatever capital I have generated till now, is from this business. I can invest all that money in construction. This is the reason my buildings are completed very fast compared to other builders. And I give quality, Sir, take my word for it. I deal face-to-face with people, because I sell personally." Ravi spoke with a little pride in his voice, but it was worth for all the hard work he had done, so I thought...

"Ravi, how many employees do you have in your company?" I asked.

"Sir, I have around thirty employees."

I was very pleased to hear this. I asked, "Oh, really! And who handles the sales department?"

"Sir, I do the selling. I have very good interaction with people. I also handle the bank transactions. I have good relations with the bank people. They give loans immediately to my customers. I have personal relations with my customers too. This formula has consistently brought deals till now.

And as you said, once you set up a formula and keep doing it again and again, you will succeed... So, at present, I have a lot of assets, mainly flats in my buildings. I have purchased some open lands from that company, who had helped me initially. I also invest in some of their good deals. Everything is going smoothly. I have ample money. My money can take care of me, my wife-to-be, my kids-to-be, as well as my other family members. My siblings are also doing well. Meanwhile, lot of things happened. My younger brother has one startup in the IT field. I share with them what you have taught me. In fact, there is a coaching class at my home in the evenings free of cost for all those who want to be entrepreneurs! Besides, I have read a lot of books, Brian Tracy, Robert Kiyosaki, Rhonda Byrne, Tony Robbins and all the other authors that you had suggested. I have attended many workshops and seminars. But the course which taught me Entrepreneurship on the court is E3; that is Entrepreneurship, Energy and Excellence." Ravi was talking non-stop.

I was more than happy to learn that he had adopted my thoughts and was imparting that knowledge to his brothers and sisters. Everything looked fine. Then what on earth had happened that made Ravi rush to me like this... I wondered. Was it the matter of heart?

I looked at him. He sensed the question in my eyes and said, "Sir, you might be thinking what brought me here today. Something has happened and I want your advice."

"Oh Ravi! Lots of things are happening in your life. From the account of the last three years, I assume that you have become financially free," I said.

"Yes, I have become financially free. Now, even if I don't work, I can live my life with the same standard of living.

If I don't create any mess-up on my own, this situation will remain in my life, because my investments are diversified as per your advice. Some of them are in gold, silver, stocks and definitely a big chunk in real estate. This is also distributed in plots, industrial lands, residential apartments, bungalows and farm-houses. Ongoing coaching from Viraj has really done wonders for me. I have a deep respect in him as a mentor. He wants to meet you. We shall meet one day."

"Sure, Ravi!" I said, "I also want to meet the guy who has transformed you so much. But, let us have some breakfast first. We will continue our talks after that."

I called our house-maid and asked her to bring the breakfast. We had omelet and cutlets with coffee. After finishing it, I said in a complaining tone to Ravi, "It is not right that once you left three years ago, you did not even call. You did not send a single email. But still I like you as you have used the aspects of business as per our discussion. I appreciate that. Okay, you were telling something about an issue which is troubling you right now. What is that?"

Chapter 9

Yes! I Am Rich Now...! But...

"Sir, everything is sailing smoothly on the family front, business front, my relations with my colleagues and family members. Only two things are not working. The second one is time management. Every day the sun rises and the sun sets. That is how this last year is gone. I hardly sleep for four to five hours," he said.

"And what is the first issue?" I asked, sensing that this one might be the urgent one.

"Sir, I told you that I attended many seminars and conferences. One conference was at Taj Palace. It was a two day seminar on Image Building and Branding. There were around 100 to 150 participants attending that conference. The trainer had started talking on the subject of personal image building. Half an hour had passed and one girl stood up with a question. I looked at her. She was stunningly beautiful and very young. The way she was talking with the trainer attracted my attention. I started to listen to her keenly."

"What did she ask?" I was curious to know.

"She asked, 'Does age really matter in personal image building in business?' I don't remember what the trainer replied, because I was just looking at her. All the people around me disappeared. I was not sitting in Taj, I was in

Dalhousie with her. I only remember her question, the way she was speaking, her body language, the green suit she was wearing, and her small specs. Her complexion was fair. I was wondering whether she was an Indian or a foreigner; this was the very first thought that came to my mind when my senses returned. Then I realized that I was in Taj." Ravi told all this in one breath.

"I decided to meet her personally and introduce myself. I eagerly waited for a break. Finally, the trainer declared a tea-break and taking a cup I started searching for her. My eyes searched for the green dress in that crowd of more than hundred, but she was not there. I thought she had left or was I dreaming about her? Was she there or not? Did she really exist?

I searched at every table and corner and finally found her! I went to her and asked, 'Excuse me ma'am, I want to talk to you for two minutes.' There was a question in her eyes. I did not pay attention to it. My heartbeats increased. 'I am really impressed by the question you asked the trainer and the way you talked, emphasizing your point regarding the age. I had never thought of that point in personal image building. May I introduce myself, I am Ravi. I am doing business in real estate. May I know who you are and what do you do?' I don't know how could I manage to speak this much. I thought, would she think me a stupid person? But, she smiled instead and said that her name was Angel and Angel Realty was her company. It struck me at once that Angel Realty was a big name in our business.

I asked a stupid question then, 'Are you working in Angel Realty?' Sir, she laughed heartily. Her white teeth sparkled like pearls. She said, 'No, no! I am the owner of Angel Realty.'

I was so astonished to hear her reply, you won't imagine! I asked in disbelief, 'Are you the owner of that company?' She said, 'Yes, I set up this company in India. Actually my father manages the European territory business and I manage the Asia-Pacific region. What do you do Mr. Ravi?' she asked in her musical voice.

I told her that I am a first generation entrepreneur. She smiled and said that she was a second generation entrepreneur. She said she was privileged that her father had already settled the business, but she was so passionate of doing the business herself that she was handling the complete Asian zone. She also told me that she was living in Mumbai since last three years.

Her voice was so sweet that it was a pleasure to hear it. I was completely engrossed and taken over by the way she was talking, by her complete personality. I could not realize what exactly attracted me towards her, was it her presence or was it the fact that she was handling so big a company at so young an age. I could not understand; but one thing was certain, her magic was working on me. By that time the break was over and we went inside. I said, 'Let us meet in the next break.' She said, 'Definitely! I like the way you are speaking and as we are from the same business, we can learn from each other.'

I don't really remember what happened in the conference after that. I could not concentrate. If you ask what the conference was about, I would say it was about the image and brand-building. The image of Angel was created inside me and the brand Angel completely established inside my heart. This is what I got from my participation in that conference. We became very good friends after that. There were a lot of phone calls, emails, WhatsApp chatting, meeting each other, going around, and hanging around. One fine day, both of us realized that we are in deep love. Not a single day passed without talking with each other. Good morning and good night messages were never skipped. Each day started with Angel and ended with Angel. We went to Himachal with some common friends this year and there in Dalhousie, I proposed to her. It was my dream to propose to her there and I used to visualize it day and night. And it came true. She accepted my proposal with pleasure."

Ravi was still in Dalhousie with his sweetheart, but I brought him back with my comment, "Then what went wrong? Everything you are telling seems fine to me..."

"Sir, I am coming to it. As I have told you, she is a very successful entrepreneur and she manages operations throughout India. I am proud of her for that. From here, she is expanding into other Asian countries. Right now, she is doing business in four other countries. She has taken a very small seed funding from her father and established a big brand like Angel Realty in Mumbai. I really appreciate that and she is a source of inspiration for me." Ravi said.

"Then what is it that brought you so early in the morning to me?" I was still not getting his point.

"Sir, you know that I handle everything in my business personally. I meet my customers, I manage construction work, and I organize meetings, conduct training workshops. I do everything on my own. I think this is the best way of doing things. My business gives me money, so I am clear about this. The issue between us is that she consistently complains that I do not have time to spend with her. And she is complaining about this throughout this last year.

She does not understand my situation and I am surprised that she doesn't, as she is also in the same business."

"Ravi, you have to give her some time. I don't see that she is asking much. This is the least expectation from a fiancé," I said.

"Sir, I tried to, but on two or three occasions I could not keep my promise and she was angry with me. One day she asked me to accompany her on a shopping spree for her father. She wanted to send him some gifts on his birthday and she said she would need my help to choose some gifts. I promised to meet her at a mall and could not keep that appointment as some clients wanted me to show them some flats. Angel was furious. She scolded me that I should appoint a manager to handle such matters." Ravi complained.

I laughed and said, "You don't know Ravi how sensitive women are about their parents' birthdays! You are not that experienced!"

Ravi said, "Not only parents, Sir. Similar incidence happened regarding one of her friends. Angel was going to attend her friend's wedding reception and she wanted me to accompany her to it. As I also knew her friend, I was also invited. But, I had a meeting with some land-holders that day and could not finish it in time. I was very late for the reception and did not have enough time to change and had to go in my working clothes, though in my opinion the attire was decent enough for that occasion, Angel did not like it. She was angry with me and said that she would not take me to any such party anymore! I somehow managed to convince her, but four days ago there was the climax."

"What happened?" I asked.

"It was her birthday, four days back. I had set up a reminder in my tab, laptop, and cell phone and with my P.A. too! I did everything to remember the day. I called her. I met her with a bouquet of red roses and chocolates. I thought I did everything perfect. She said then, 'I have arranged a party at the Taj, where we met for the first time. So, I want you to be there at seven in the evening. I want to declare our engagement to all my friends.' I said okay and we parted. I had a slab casting that day on the seventh floor in one of my new townships on Nasik-Mumbai highway. And three customers were going to book in one of my projects that day. I thought I would easily finish my work by 5 o'clock and attend the party at seven. But, the slab casting did not finish in time and the three persons also could not adhere to their appointment in time. So, I was already late and on the top of that, I got stuck in the evening traffic. I tried to call her, but she did not receive my calls. I somehow managed to reach at the hotel, but it was too late. The party was over, as it was nearly midnight. Angel was there, tears rolling down her cheeks and eyes blazing with anger. I instantly knew what I was going to face. She refused to listen to my apologies and said, 'Now, our relationship is over. I can't even think of marrying a man like you who doesn't bother to care about me and my feelings. You better take care of your business and your money.' I tried to stop her. I pleaded from the bottom of my heart. But she went without listening to me. I called her in the night and asked to meet her, but she refused and we fought over the phone.

I could not sleep that night. Next day, she might have felt that she had behaved very rudely with me, so she called me and we met. She said, 'If you are going to do business in this fashion, you will never succeed. You have to put your business on automatic mode, my father has taught me so. I am also in this business, I also construct buildings; but the difference is I have never attended a single slab casting on my site. Still my business is growing. I have tried to discuss with you all this, but you never listened. You only listen to that guy, that Guru of yours. Go and talk to him. And if you come back with something worth telling which appeals to me, then and then only will I consider whether to continue our relationship or not. If you will be able to convince me, I will take you to meet my parents. Give me some plan that gives not only money to you, but provides ample time to make use of that money and enjoy life. Your business is giving you money right now, but it is not giving me anything. If you can come up with something which really will make our seven generations ultra-rich, then I will be interested, because I am also from an Indian origin.'"

I interrupted Ravi, "But you told me she was a foreigner?"

"Her father is an Indian, settled in Spain and got married to a Spanish lady." Ravi said. "They live in Barcelona and she was born and brought up there. She always says that they live with Indian values and the western working culture. She tells me that I work like a donkey and can't find time for anything other than work. She says that she has studied the working cultures of the Indians and the Westerners. According to her, we Indians think about business twenty-four hours and are not able to enjoy the fruits of our toil. We don't have a five day week in many organizations and spend the weekend in next week's planning. We always think about money and not comfort. We go for shopping half heartedly, always worrying about our purse. In her opinion, Indians don't respect women entrepreneurs, though Indian women have immense ability of entrepreneurship in them. India needs a leader who stands for women entrepreneurs. The people of the western countries, on the contrary, enjoy life. They go on short trips on the weekends, they shop, and they eat whatever they want, without worrying about the upcoming week. They refresh their mind and body and are ready to face the next five days of hard work. She says that we Indians never concentrate fully on our work while working and never enjoy whole-heartedly our free time."

"What she said is hundred per cent true, Ravi," I appreciated the young lady's analysis. She was very clear about her priorities. Ravi would be a lucky chap, if he would manage to win her heart, I thought. The Wealth Guru in me was very pleased with her approach to life. "So, that is why you are here. That young lady has sent you to me; otherwise you had forgotten me, uh?" I teased him.

"Sir, please don't pull my legs. I am already on my knees before her. I also went to my mentor Viraj. He gave me some tips, but he is so busy. He said that if you stop working, money will stop coming to you. I am confused by the contradictory arguments from her and Viraj. What is the use of all this money if there is no honey like Angel in my life?" Ravi sat there before me, his head hanging down again like three years back. Here was the same young man, now rich with money but in the shadow of fear of losing the most precious gem of his life... His sweetheart!

I was trying to grasp the situation. I summed up it like this...

Angel liked Ravi; it was evident from his story. Now, why did she like him? Because, he was a first generation entrepreneur and she was a second generation entrepreneur, which she did not like much and had complaints being so. Her father had asked her to do certain things in a certain way and that bothered her. She wanted to have her own way of doing things. This fact sometimes upset her.

At the same time, she tries to communicate some real good facts regarding business that she has learnt from her father and appreciates them. But, Ravi is not paying any attention to her suggestions, as he wants to do things in his own way. That is the only thing that upsets her about Ravi. His behavior is not satisfactory in her opinion and she wants him to amend some of his business habits. That is all.

And I thought I would be able to solve this issue, as a Wealth Guru.

Chapter 10

Entrepreneurship and Leadership

I looked up from my thoughts at Ravi. He was now looking expectantly at me, waiting for me to say something.

I said, "Ravi, I had cautioned you three years ago and advised you not to make haste again, but you didn't take my advice seriously. Let it be; past is past. Let us move ahead. I comprehend everything now, your situation, your dilemma… everything. I have enough experience as a Wealth Guru to deal with such situations. So, don't worry, we will come up with some kind of solution. I promise you that, when you will leave this farm-house of mine, you will go with your peace of mind restored and promise of a happy future."

"I now have a crystal clear idea of the whole situation and I can visualize how to create what you really want to create. You will get Angel," I consoled him. "See Ravi, it is not only about becoming ultra-rich. It is about building a seven–star business which will last for the next seven generations. And for that, we will discuss about the next four aspects of entrepreneurship." I said to him.

As Ravi had jumped upon me unexpectedly in the morning, I was not ready for this appointment. Actually,

I had decided to spend the whole week at the farm-house doing nothing; but looking at Ravi and the situation he was facing, prompted me to cancel my vacation and return to the city and work. So, I told him to come to my office the next day and there we would start our discussion.

Ravi left, taking my leave and promise, to meet at my office on Wednesday – that is, the next day.

It was 9 o'clock on Wednesday morning. My intercom rang and the receptionist told me it was Ravi. I asked her to let him in. He entered the cabin and shook hands with me. I greeted, asked him to have a seat and started talking,

"Ravi, let us start with the topic 'entrepreneurship and leadership'. First of all, we will look at what is entrepreneurship, but before that, we will have to look at what does it mean to be an entrepreneur. Entrepreneur is someone who is always at risk and entrepreneurship is creating a risk for you by playing something which is really big, which is mega, and facing all those challenges using the various theories. As an entrepreneur you have to learn to either walk on that pathway or do various things that are already in the life. That is entrepreneurship. An entrepreneur is someone who is out there in the world to make the difference. An entrepreneur is someone who comes up with some idea, builds the whole business around that idea, takes it to the new level and makes it available to more and more people."

Now, it was my turn to talk and Ravi's to listen! He was listening very carefully.

I continued, "An entrepreneur is someone who gives employment to hundreds or thousands or millions of people and entrepreneurship is actually what people can see through your business-building. Each one of us wants to be a successful entrepreneur and you also want to become one. Do you want to be successful, so that your next seven generations can enjoy that success? Then the key aspect for that is Leadership. Entrepreneurship and Leadership go hand in hand when it comes to business. The term 'Leadership' is derived from the word 'Leader'. Who is a leader? From the context of business, a leader is someone who plays a key role in business. He is the nucleus of business. He is the source.

A leader is someone who leads from the front. Where does he lead? He leads on the court. What is a court? Here, entrepreneurship is the court and the leader leads on the court of entrepreneurship. Leaders demonstrate leadership consistently and continuously in entrepreneurship. He knows when to lead and when to follow. He knows when to speak and when to listen. A leader knows how to lead people and how to follow them. He knows when to do what. He knows when to take action and when to hold back."

Ravi said, "Sir, please speak more about leadership."

"A leader knows about leadership. He knows leadership as a concept and leadership as a phenomenon. He can visualize the future. A leader is someone who can see at least ten years ahead. Leader is someone who motivates people. A leader is someone who inspires others. Any business requires an entrepreneur who is a leader. People should get inspiration by merely remembering a leader or just looking at either his photograph or image or him in person. A leader walks what he talks. He or she should lead from the front. He should be an icon, an idol for his followers. There is one proverb which says, 'Action speaks louder than words'.

Why do we want to develop leadership and entrepreneurship? It is because our mission is to create a business which will last for the next seven generations.

The aspect of leadership is 'Self-Discipline'.

When I say self, I mean you, Ravi. For you as a business person, self-discipline is the most important quality for any leader. People follow the leader. People follow the business owner. Self-discipline begins with thinking in a certain way, visualizing the things in a certain way and acting in certain way.

It is also related to commitment and delivery. When you say I will be there for a meeting at ten, you have to be there at ten, ready to start the meeting. Many leaders are so punctual that when they enter the office, the wall clock says, 'now it is the time!' Self-discipline also has the aspect of commitment and delivery.

You have to be very honest and truthful in business. 'Honesty ad Transparency' is the next aspect. Honesty and Transparency are those qualities that every individual should posses for that matter and they are extremely important for a leader. When your employees see that you are honest, they work for you. When you do business deals with some other people, who are not your followers, they will not like to work for you unless they see honesty in you. If they sense any discrepancies in you, they will not work for you honestly.

The next aspect is 'Being Responsible'."

"Sir, but most of the people behave responsibly," Ravi interfered.

"Yes Ravi, but when I say 'responsible', I mean that the person is the sole cause behind all the following activities.

He should think, 'this is my business. This is my life.' And he should say, 'I wanted to create all this.' Nobody came and forced you Ravi to do this... You said and right now you have achieved a lot. Actually you are already financially free for this generation and the next generation also, but right now, you say you are willing to create something which is bigger than this, right?"

"Very true Sir," Ravi said, "That is why I am here for your guidance."

"For that you have to be very responsible," I said. "The responsibility begins with the willingness of being the cause in the matter of life, being the cause in the matter of business and being the cause in the matter of the people concerned in the business. I say this for all those relevant parties which are part of your business and responsible for that. Responsibility is not a burden. Responsibility is an opportunity to take the matter in your own hands and show the world what you can do. It is an opportunity to prove you. Responsibility is really creating a mega business, really doing all the day to day activities with ease and grace, because your peace of mind is your responsibility and you are responsible for that, as you can't be clear in your mind about the ideas unless your mind is peaceful."

"What is the next principle?" Ravi asked.

"The next principle is 'listening'.

"As a successful leader, as a successful entrepreneur, the listening ability is the key. Basically, human beings don't listen. Many people are not good listeners... Human beings listen to something which is their version of what the other person says, and this creates lots of confusion and misunderstandings in the organization. When we work in an organization, we have to work with people, deal with them. The same thing applies to our relationships too, not only in office or business.

Since long Angel is trying to tell you something but you are not listening. You are listening to your version of that. Your version is this that 'She is trying to enforce something on me'. You want to do it in your way, but if you listen to her keenly and understand what she is trying to convey, then you can get the true meaning. Listening is the key. If you listen carefully you can speak with authority. You can speak with confidence. Whatever you say, people will listen. When you listen to others, others will listen to you. It is like give and take."

Ravi said, "That means, keeping all senses open, right? I like this principle!"

"Yes Ravi, you are right there!" I said. "The next aspect is 'keeping all senses open'.

Being an entrepreneur, being a leader, when we are dealing with people, walking through life, walking through the various aspects of business, we don't need any superpower or any external force to get it done through ourselves. Nothing is required. Ravi, if you participate by keeping all your senses open; be cautious, you will understand what's happening around you. A successful leader and entrepreneur is someone who always gets or collects information as the business owner.

If you are listening to people, one of the senses you are using is listening. You are actually seeing what is there. Most of the time, we try to see what's not there. People use the word intuition, but my perception about intuition is the information you gather through all those awakened senses. The information you gather through all those five senses, which are at the upper most level of awareness, gives you some input… That gives you the major input to take any decision. As a business owner, you have to be very decisive, and you have to take many decisions while you move on in business. This power of keeping all senses open helps in taking the decisions.

Now I will talk about one of the most important aspect and that is 'playing big'," I said.

"Why is it so important?" Ravi asked.

"Thinking small and playing small is a crime. If you are going to do something, why should you do it for millions? Why not do it for billions? You will require the same effort and the same pathway to create billions. You have to use all these sutras for being a millionaire or a billionaire, then why not to be a billionaire? Why to serve only Asia and Europe? Why not to serve all the seven continents? Think big. Most of the Indian entrepreneurs, they think about ten crores. The magic figure of most of the Indian entrepreneurs I've met is hundred crores. I say that, if they begin any startup in this country, if they begin their plan from thinking about 10,000 crores, then that can shift the whole economy of this country. If they succeed or fail, at least they will achieve the figure of 100 crores.

Then, India can be the financial superpower of the world. My humble request to you is just play it really big. Plan accordingly. You know now how to plan and all the things related to it. We have talked a lot earlier. Create something which is mega. Create something which is big. So, imagine how many people you can serve.

When you are working from your town, your view of the world is limited. You look up to an influential person in your town and get impressed by his achievement and wish to become like him. You want to play the business game like him. Yes! I say 'business is a game of wins and losses'. If you fail in one game you should move on to play the next game. When you look at that person in the context of the country, he would not seem so big. And when you go outside the country, your perspective changes and it widens. You look at things in a different view. An entrepreneur should always think globally. Making the business global while keeping the roots local is the real key. A real successful Indian entrepreneur is the one who is having global vision with very strong local roots. This is the true meaning of 'playing big'!

The next aspect is 'dealing with failure.'

Ravi, shall I tell you about failure?" I asked with amusement.

He also responded with a smile. This time he did not hang his head down. He had now taken his failure in his stride and moved ahead.

"You've already experienced that right? At that time also I said if one is not enough, second is there. If second is not enough, there is the third too… keep doing. Keep doing, till the time you succeed or die. That's the only way to deal with failure. Don't give up! There is not a single entrepreneur in this world who has not failed; but a true entrepreneur never gives up. Only successful people face failures in life. Only successful people go through the failures but how you deal with the failure is the key for opening the door of new opportunities. Failure is the biggest teacher. Failure is the biggest coach. Failure is the real Guru. Failure is the real mentor. How you deal with the failure is important and that's where the leadership comes and that's where the entrepreneurship comes. That's where all the above-said sutras will help you in dealing with that failure because after every failure, there is a breakthrough bigger than that failure or at least at the level of the failure. Most of the time, the breakthrough is bigger than that failure."

"If you can keep your senses sharp and alert, you can sense the opportunity that is hidden in that failure. A true entrepreneur is the person who deals with the adverse situation and while keeping all the above-said aspects in mind and working from the experiences, uses them as a context and walks on the pathway of success. He is the true leader."

"Sir, what you are sharing with me is of great value. Now I can see what mistakes I was doing," Ravi said.

I smiled and said, "Ravi, there are a few more aspects which remain to be discussed. We will meet tomorrow…" I said.

Ravi took my leave and went away.

Chapter 11

Building a Winning Team

Next day we met in my office again and started our discussion.

"What has happened till date with you is, you are doing everything on your own. You are getting huge success by doing it by yourself. So you are getting so many pay-offs on you by doing it on your own. One of them is you are already financially free." I started the next session after we took tea.

"You have people working with you. There is a brand. Already your organization is a brand. This is the pay-off you have got because you have established yourself as a brand and you have set up yourself as an established entrepreneur. That's why you have a girlfriend or fiancée with you." I smiled and looked at Ravi. He smiled back at me. The fear of losing Angel was vanishing slowly from his face. He looked less tense now.

I continued, "The other pay-offs are for supporting your family, and some good friends of yours. So, you have already got some name and fame. You have achieved all this on your own and by consistent hard work. But my friend, you are paying a huge cost for it and what's that cost? You are achieving all this at the cost of love, affinity, health and vitality and deep sleep. You are not getting the vital gains.

The thing which hurts you at present is Angel. She said something and you were disturbed by it. That's why you are here. Otherwise you would not have come to me. According to me, you have to earn time... If you ask me the importance of time, time is money but it's not in the sense that of how much time you save. It's actually how much other people's time you buy. The time people give to you for your organizational growth. That's the key. OPT, Other People's Time!"

"What should I do to improve this?" Ravi asked.

"You have people working with you, but you are doing it on your own and that's why you don't have time. That's why your girlfriend is suffering and you are on the verge of a break- up. It's directly making an impact on your health and vitality. Is that the cost you are paying, my friend? That's why we need peace because if you are full of love and you are experiencing peace of mind, only then you can be ultra-rich in a systemized way... in an affordable manner which will be good for all. You are wearing branded shirts. Did the owner of that company come to you to sell those shirts? No! If you delegate the work then automatically you will get free time."

Ravi nodded.

"You have to create a team and there are benefits of working with a team. Most of the time people like you may think that I alone can do it best. It's good to be a perfectionist. Being a self-employed person, it's good to be a perfectionist. But when we are building a business which will last for the next seven generations, we have to focus on growth rather than perfection. If you focus on growth, perfection will happen automatically and if there are experts, a team of dedicated people, a team of people like you who are completely convinced with the vision and mission of the organization, then your business will grow effectively with perfection. Creating such a team is the key. That's why right now I am explaining to you the importance of building a winning team. You have people around you; but do you have right people at right positions?

We are not only talking about building a team. We are talking about building a winning team. A winning team is the team which takes the organization where it intends to go. Winning team is a team which delivers all the desired results. It's a group of people working together consistently and continuously for the vision and mission of the organization. Winning team is a team of people working for the leader. Winning team is a team of people who keep all their personal concerns aside and work for the customers or the stakeholders and for all the relevant parties of the organization. That's the true winning team according to me."

"How does the winning team look on the court? Is it possible in real life; in real business?" Ravi seemed doubtful.

"If you are the only brilliant person in your team you are in trouble Ravi. You are really in trouble, because our brain has limitations. Having more and more people who are brilliant like you and bringing them into the team is the key," I said.

"Now I realize what Angel was trying to convey to me," Ravi said thoughtfully, "Sir, guide me in how I can build a winning team."

"That's it!" I said, "Now you are on the right track. We will look at the first principle of building a winning team.

Right now, you have one private limited company right? So, if you really want to be ultra-rich and if you choose your company to be private limited, public limited, or limited liability partnership, you will need some experts in your team.

So, the first team according to me for the whole organization to be rich for the next seven generations or to sustain for the next seven generations, is the team of owners. Or I'll say, when the company has a board of directors, the team is the key team. They are the source of the organization. The way they behave, the way they act, the way they think seeps down to the organization. These are very important people. But, right now, you are the only one. I don't know if you like partnerships or not, but if you ask me, my first suggestion to you is, there must be at least four or five board members." I suggested.

"What do the board members do?" Ravi asked.

"Board members are the people who are solely responsible for bringing the vision and mission of the organization into reality. Board members are a team of people who know what to do and what not to. Board members are the team of people who are solely accountable for all the desired results. Board members are a team of people for whom the organization is greater than their personal interests. Board members are the people who may be stakeholders, shareholders of that company or may not be. There are independent directors too. They are someone who says we are responsible for what is happening in this organization. If the customer is not getting a good service they are responsible for that."

"Now, I am realizing my mistake. I tried to do everything by myself and so there was no other thought in my mind other than business and customers. I would always try to prove that I do everything very efficiently and that effort would leave me exhausted." Ravi confessed.

"Very true Ravi. You would feel much relaxed when you would form this team of owners. They basically stand together. They are one. They do whatever is needed and necessary and whatever it takes to grow the organization."

"Who are the board members? How to find them?" Ravi asked.

"Look around you; at least you'll get one or two board members. Get the support of your friends; you can call some friends, some good friends of yours. You can even bring any business person who has already created a big business. You can request that person and bring him on your team of board members." I said.

"What next? I think I have to do a lot of searching…" He said.

"Yes Ravi, you will have to. Now, let us look at the team of mentors. I am talking about the team of mentors because on your pathway of growth you need various types of mentors. Right now, you have this mentor of yours, what is his name?"

"Viraj Chaudhari," Ravi replied.

"Yes, now I remember! Viraj Chaudhari is someone who is a perfect self-employed, successful business person. He has taught you so many things and that's why you have succeeded but you have also become a typical self-employed person who doesn't have any time. You have a lot of money but no time, no time for self and no time for others. You have stuck to your business 24 × 7, isn't it?" I asked.

"Yes Sir, you are right. I can see now what went wrong and what I should have done before. But, I have a question, who would agree to become my mentor and why?" he asked doubtfully.

"If you really want to be someone who is ultra-rich having a lot of time, you must find out someone as a mentor who is living this life. I'm not saying this is very easy to do. You can find such people, you can meet such people. You can find out at least one for yourself. Such successful people, most of them are contributors. They also want to create support and nurture the entrepreneurs like you. There may be only one mentor or there may be more than one mentor. It's your choice. There are some people whom you can make your mentor only for your specific business. This is about creating a team of mentors. But, how should this mentor be? Ravi, a mentor is someone who asks you to do something which you really don't want to do and don't like to do. Why does he or she ask you to do this? Because only by doing that, can you reach where you really intend to reach. That's why they ask you to do all the stuff which you have not done in your life earlier, that's why you're stuck where you're stuck."

"A mentor is someone who looks from a helicopter; he's having that helicopter view. He is someone who is concerned about your growth and about your organization's growth. Mentor is someone who is desperate to contribute. Mentor is someone who is a successful person. Mentor is someone who tells the mentee what to do and what not to do. Mentor is someone who shows the torch in the dark. He shows the path. Mentor is someone whom you give due respect and someone you are afraid of. Mentor is someone who sometimes may not be a very successful person."

"And what is my role in all this?" Ravi asked.

"As a mentee, your job is to take all those feedback. Mentor is someone who gives proper feedback at proper time to his mentee and a mentee's job is taking all those feedback positively and learning from it and forwarding to self and to the organization. There is also one aspect about the mentors. The relationship between the mentor and the mentee must be so transparent, so clear that a mentee must share all the breakthroughs and breakdowns in business. It's like going to an advocate and a doctor. Without exactly sharing the problem, the mentor cannot make a difference in your life. A mentor is not a king but he is a king-maker.

As a Wealth Guru, people always come and ask me, not only you Ravi, but many other businessmen… They ask me, "What's the best HR management? How can I retain my people? How can I get the best out of them?

Keep aside all the management theories for the moment, but as a business owner, your job is to love people. The employees understand that language other than any other training. If they sense it, they will work for you for generations. Love is the key phenomenon in dealing with people."

"Sir, you are making the whole picture so clear that now I come to know why people call you Wealth Guru," Ravi said.

"When people work together, there are some misunderstandings, there are certain grievances; but that is natural. It happens in our family too. The reason I emphasize this factor of love more is because, most of the employees pay more time in the organization than at home. If the atmosphere in your organization is homely, automatically their performance increases. You don't have to ask them to perform. Creating an ambience, creating an atmosphere of love, compassion and an ambience like home automatically attracts employees towards their work.

Everyone loves to be appreciated. If each employee feels, 'I am valued enough, my organization needs me', then this sense of need itself keeps people intact and this creates the winning team.

Major part of the organization will come from that age group of between thirty and forty. Now, it's your job Ravi to understand their world, what they do, what they like, what they want.

Ravi, you might be thinking I have to do a lot of things to be ultra-rich or to build a business which will last for the next seven generations. Yes, my friend. Lots of things are to be done, but it is necessary to take that very first baby step in doing all these things. Actually, the key is mastering the entrepreneurship, and how can you master anything, do you know? It begins with the very first baby step. Keep doing it. And then keep doing it. Keep doing it. By practice, the muscles get developed, and then it starts happening automatically. That is mastery. You don't have to do something. It is getting done through the entire team. This also applies for all these business sutras. Initially, you will feel as if you have to do very hard work to achieve all these things that I have told you; but it's not. It's all about understanding your need and then doing it step by step.

Now, we are going to talk about the team of investors. When I say investors, I mean various types of investors. Banks, financial institutions, private investors, venture capitalists, private equity funds and other international players. All these are investors. So creating a team of investors is very important, because for any business, you need money for growth, and at all the stages there is need of money. The amount may vary, but there is need of money and who is the best business person, do you know? One who raises funds when it's necessary and also when they are not needed immediately.

The excess funds will work as a pressure for you; pressure for growth. If you have ample amount of money just lying aside, you'll create something out of it. That's the key. So this is about the need of the money.

Now we'll look at the investors. What does an investor want? Investor is someone who understands the whole language of investing. He wants the return on his investment, and most of them want sound amounts as returns. So, first they want their capital to be secured. Nobody wants that I'll invest this much amount of money, and after a period of time all my money evaporates. Nobody wants that. Each one of us wants sound returns on our investments. The same thing applies to the investors.

Investors are people; their money works for them. So, as a business person, some of our ventures really do well. Some do best. A few don't, right? And some perform average. A very few can even make losses. In the face of all these, create a pool of investors. A team of investors is very important and for that, you have to give returns to the investors consistently. If you lose money in any of your ventures along with your investors, you again have to take care of them and give them opportunity to invest in some very good business and compensate them. Making up the losses and compensating for them is part and parcel of any business.

There is another team; the team of consultants!

A consultant is someone who shows you the right direction when you are in a dilemma. He helps you to attain a result of some targeted task and he is proficient enough for doing this. You may need such type of people sometimes for the long term, but you cannot depend on your employees for that. The consultants actually support your team. Some of my friends jokingly say that a consultant is someone who takes your watch and shows you the exact time and asks for his fees for that! Jokes apart, a few of them are like this, but we need them.

Who are in this team? There are chartered accountants. There are company secretaries. There are branding consultants. There are ISO consultants. There are HR consultants; some training consultants; intellectual property consultants, etc. etc. Then there are financial consultants, and so many, and so on. So these are the consultants, and if you have a powerful team of consultants who support the whole organization in the growth, you will walk the path of success. Actually, they walk along with you on this path.

So, creating partnership with consultants will help you immensely. Convincing them with your vision and mission will set you free. You will not need to work on them after that. They will work on their own along with your team. This team is the key team which you need actually right now. They will make you free."

"What are the other benefits?" Ravi asked.

"Your brain is working out a lot of ideas. Access them when you're working in the business. Your employees aren't working in the business. They might not get access to those ideas but the consultants bring in new ideas. Sometimes they might be the rays of hope. They bring in new aspects which will enhance the entire productivity of the team. These are some of the examples, and some of the benefits that consultants will bring.

What is the benefit to an organization? Yes, this is a good question! A consultant is the master of that particular task. Chartered accountant knows what profit is, what loss is, what the balance sheet is. He is the master of that. So, what you have to do is to hire the best-suited person for that role. You will have to pay handsomely to obtain quality work. If you pay peanuts, then only monkeys will come to you!

Ravi, building a team is not an easy task overall, but it's simple. Again, you have to create the whole blueprint for creating these teams, along with the targets and the action plan. If you use all your five senses and do your business, you will get the answer for when to create which team and to realize which team is immediately needed. All this planning is required to create the big organization."

"Yes Sir, I will have to do lots of planning first..." Ravi agreed.

"Never ever forget that team consists of individuals. Individual has his or her own ego; his or her own strengths; his or her own weakness; his or her own aura. As a business person, our job is to understand the human design, and what each individual really wants. Most of us want the things which actually don't cost anything. Like happiness, joy, fun and love. This is what humans ultimately want. They want a peace of mind. Understanding the human design is the key and if you are able to give that in your organization, you can attract all the good people like a magnet. You will be a magnet attracting good people to your organization. You will ask, 'Is this really possible?' Yes, this is possible!" I said.

"Individuals acting in their own way will not form a team, but ten individuals working as a team will make the difference... What's team? Team is individuals working together with complete oneness. When we see from outside, we can see that they're acting as a team. If you see the paramilitary forces, the way they walk, the way they behave, the way they pull their guns. There is oneness. This whole team acts as one. When they are pulling their weapons, they are pulling while acting in synchronization.

Individuals working together with oneness of heart and mind, and acting in synchronization can create miracles for any organization. You can see the miracle in the form of results and you can see the results from the balance sheets of that organization.

Does each individual working in a team actually contribute to the balance sheet of the organization? As a business person, it is your job to make sure that this happens. Growth of individual also matters. It is the job of the business owner to take care of each individual's growth. The real key in this is taking care of the people working under us and training them to take care of the down line.

Taking care of each individual ultimately will take much effort. All the teams will get support and they will grow. As the team grows, the individual grows, as the individual grows, the team grows, and as the team grows, the oneness gets boosted and as the level of oneness elevates, again the synchronization goes to the optimum level and miraculous growth happens. This is the real key of team building."

Ravi was not tired of listening; but I was of talking continuously for three hours. So, we decided to take a break and meet the next day.

Chapter 12

System of Systems

My intercom rang the next day at 9 o'clock and I knew it was Ravi! He entered my cabin, greeted me and handed me a set of bottles of massage oils. I smiled and said, "You implement my teachings and become successful; that is enough for me as a Wealth Guru!"

Ravi said, "Sir, I can offer you only this at present. It is nothing compared to what you are giving me. Your advice is more valuable to me than anything. And, do not take my gifts otherwise; I am offering to you out of sheer love and respect."

"Thank you Ravi! Shall we start our discussion?" I asked and he nodded.

"We are now going to discuss about creating a 'system'. Basically, there is a system everywhere. Our homes also have some kind of system; but it is not a written system. It is an unsaid system. Similarly, every business has its own system. Small organizations have oral system or rules while big or mega organizations have written systems and rules. They are a must. A system works like glue. It holds the whole organization together, including all the stakeholders. In very simple words, a process which is set to achieve all the targets and all the goals of the organization is called system.

As you know, system is one of the very important aspects of business. How to set a system and exactly what type of system do you have to set? It is necessary to set up a system in a business in which you as an entrepreneur are not required to run the business. As an entrepreneur, your job is to go to the next level of making the seven generations rich and taking the whole business to the next orbit. Your job is not to work in the business; instead your job is to work on the business. And for that, you have to set up a system which doesn't require you, and which can be run without your presence and not only for a year, but for years. Even if you're not there, the business would be growing and achieving all the targets. We are talking here about a business that will last for the next seven generations."

"But how is it possible?" Ravi asked.

"This is the real game and we will see how to do this.

First of all, you have to set up a system which will run all the systems in the organization. I will tell you the story of my American friend who has established a system of systems and now he is enjoying the fruits of his efforts. This friend of mine has a bungalow on the sea shore. I'm really jealous of him. What he likes is the sea. He is having a seafront villa. What does he do? He sits there in his balcony with a notepad kept aside, some pencils and papers. He just looks at all the waves of the sea and whatever comes to his mind, he just scribbles it down on that notepad. Somebody comes, takes that notepad and creates the things for him which he intends to create for his business. Sometimes it may be a new business idea. Sometimes there may be ideas about his existing business. Sometimes, there may be ideas for serving the customers. When he gets bored at looking at the waves, he takes his yacht and goes deep into the sea and thinks I can scribble down something there and he comes back. Somebody takes the notepad from the yacht and does whatever he intends to deliver. Why this friend of mine is having peace of mind is because earlier he has put so many years developing this system, connecting those brilliant people, connecting all the gems and bringing all the gems into his team. That's what he has done in the past. That's why he is living in such a fashion today.

Creating such a system is the real brain game. There're various consultants who will help you in this. If you put more hours in creating such a system and brainstorm with your team, you can create a system which will keep you free. You can handle your business from any part of the world. Though you are away from your business, whenever you want a feedback it's available for you, and it's by your choice. For that, you have to make someone from your team a system-head. He will fix the various responsibilities with auditing, accounting, infrastructure, human resources, etc. He will chalk up who will do what and how.

You will be enjoying your life; you will be doing whatever you're doing. Right now, you have to compromise with many of your relationships, your family, your friends, your relatives and some business friends to reach to this place, because you're not giving them the quality time, or the quantity time. Now the time has come to set up a system which will run the organization, which will grow the organization, which will achieve all the targets of the organization without you being there, so that you can do whatever you intend to do. That's the real game.

Setting up a system for any of your products or services, where consistent maintenance from the organization is not needed, is the important task. Everything should be fulfilled automatically and working 24 × 7 × 365. If you're not making more money while you are sleeping, then I can say assuredly that you're going to be poor. That's the real game; that is, creating a system which is going to work automatically.

System requires people, business requires people. What do we do when we get a repeated order from the same customer? We're so happy, and our sales team is also happy, right? We're happy that the same vendor is again serving us. Here I'm talking about connecting these people for the next seven generations, all your vendors, all your shareholders, all your employees, and all your customers. Think it from a domain of connecting them for the next seven generations, and creating a system to connect them for the next seen generations. Nobody has thought about it. I think this is the first time and Ravi; you will not get this in any of the books. We are distinguishing systems from our very different world view; nobody has given it a thought yet. I am sharing this with you for the first time!

You have to think over how to create a system, or connect people and connecting them for the next seven generations. If you really want to be ultra-rich for the next seven generations, create a system, which will make each individual rich, each individual who is part of your business and all the relevant parties in your business; your employees, your suppliers, your vendors, your customers, etc. Set up a system creating a business model in such a way that all the relevant parties will become rich.

If all the relevant parties are getting rich, you'll not have to worry about your own richness, they will make you rich. You know how this happens. If you are really concerned about the society, the cults, and the communities and if your product, your service is really making a difference to the grass root level of that community, or that society, or the people of that country, all of them will want you. You don't have to push marketing. All of them will do it for you. People pull the products towards them; you don't have to push it. This is so very simple; it happens. You have to keep doing this and keep doing this for a period of time, and then you'll automatically be ultra-rich.

Here, I'm talking about creating a system where new ideas from all the classes, from all the stakeholders are received. I am talking about creating a system, and getting new ideas inside, working on whichever are relevant; creating an automatic system for new ideas and innovations, maybe some inventions, and getting all these things inside, nurturing those, creating a system for that, executing it again either for creating a new business or connecting those ideas, those inventions, or those innovations to the existing business. That's the system I'm talking about.

It's just an idea of two communities operating together and nothing else. The communities are already there. I am not inventing any new idea; this is just a simple idea of connecting two communities. Actually in most of the organizations, any office peon, any machine-operator may have certain ideas; and they sometimes know better, what will work better, but there is no system in the organization for communicating their ideas. In some organizations, there are systems, but nobody really listens to that guy, and who knows, that can be a multimillion dollar idea!"

"Yes, now I understand!" Ravi said with satisfaction.

"The next aspect is about the 'leader creation system'.

Right now, I think, we have created the four-tier system of the team. There's the advisory team, the board of directors, the employees, and the senior level management. The organization needs leaders at various levels and many times there are good people inside the organizations; but there is no such concrete system in many organizations to create support and nurture the leaders. You should create a system of creative leaders who will achieve all the desired goals of the organization at various levels. Create a system which will last for the next seven generations; because after a period of time, it becomes routine for the people working there. New people, youngsters coming inside can bring new talent, but the youngsters might not have the culture and the values of any senior person who is working with you.

Actually when a youngster comes and joins any organization and he retires, either he goes to another organization after a period of time, or a supplier who is your leader, gets some opportunity to go out in a different organization, and that's why he doesn't want to be with you; then what happens? This is what actually I want to talk about. I am not only talking about this passing on to the next generation, I'm talking about creating a system which will create leaders in all the aspects. Create leaders in customers. They will become your brand ambassador for the next seven generations.

The last but not the least aspect of the system is fulfillment. According to me, the system should be such where everyone lives a complete life. When I say complete life, I mean a life full of love, joy, prosperity, family, fulfillment and peace of mind. Create a system where all the relevant parties and all the concerned people of your organizations experience peace of mind, fulfillment, love, joy, and happiness. You can think about a system where all the people in one section meet their team-leader once in a week and give their feedback. You can create a system of doing an 'Omkara' chanting at the beginning of the office hours; or inviting a 'Yoga' teacher on Sundays to teach 'Yoga' to the employees. You can arrange a Diwali get-together or an annual gathering for the employees. In this way, you can create a bonding between the management and the employees."

Chapter 13

Making a Difference

"Sir," Ravi asked, "How can I get the sense of fulfillment through my work? Now I consider that it is the more important thing than money and other worldly gains."

"Ravi, the sense of fulfillment comes from helping others. This is a natural human instinct to give support to others. Humans love to help others. But, sometimes they forget this instinct in their day to day grind. A true social worker is he, who after becoming rich donates a part of his income to the needy people in the society."

"Ravi," I said, "We don't know from where we have come and where we will go. We have this short life span of seventy to seventy-five years in between. We should think, whether I am making advancement in every aspect of life? We go after a few specific things, like money, work, relationships, etc.; instead, we should live a complete life," I said.

"Ravi, you know the names of many billionaires in the world, from Warren Buffett to Bill Gates to Mark Zuckerburg. What did they do after becoming ultra-rich? What did they do? They donated most of their fortunes to the society. This is the trend which really began with Henry Ford." I said.

"Yes Sir, I have read about them and have immense respect for them," Ravi said.

"Henry Ford invented the first car, created big fortunes for himself, and then he established the Ford Foundation. After Henry Ford passed away, the Ford Foundation is making a lot of difference out there in the world till date. But what really inspires me is that, after getting to be ultra-rich they gave a certain amount from their profit back to the society. But can this be planned early? Have you heard of Manoj Bhargava, an American citizen of Indian origin? He planned in this way. He recently became a billionaire by selling the 5-hour energy drink.

He sold all those at gas stations and in the convenience stores in the United States and he became a billionaire out of that. He invented new products, really innovative. It is invention. He created a bicycle; by pedaling it for one hour, it will give electricity for twenty-four hours to any house. He converted sea water into a usable water bottle for irrigation purposes. He created a machine which looked like a body massage machine and he created something which makes any person healthy. After getting a lot of money, he thought, 'what will I do with all this money?'

He donated 99 percent of his wealth to the society and created such a product for the society which will really benefit the last person of the pyramid and which will have global impact, which will have impact on a very large scale and which will bring sustainability in the environment. I think this kind of work makes difference in the world and for an entrepreneur having ample funds, this is easily possible.

A real Indian way of doing social work is contributing some part of your wealth to fulfill your passion towards the needy people. Indians have a softer corner for the social causes than other people in the world, as I think. It is in our ancient culture to give water and food to the needy. No one should go empty handed is the teaching of our ancestors," I said.

"Sir, but what if I don't give back to the society? Is it necessary to do so?" Ravi asked.

"See Ravi, as a successful business person, you have a choice of giving it back to the society or not; but ask yourself, will you be happy by giving it back? If the answer is no, then don't give it back. If the answer is yes, then do it and do it in your own way. There are so many organizations, and the corporate entities have created systemized structures to giving it back to the society. I shared with you the story of Manoj Bhargava. That is his way of contributing to the society. That's his way of making a difference. That's his way of giving it back to the society,

In India, there are organizations like the Tatas … Their purpose is giving it back to the society while doing business. That's why I respect them the most. I don't remember the name of the organization, but the owner of that organization said, 'We don't make profit to just make the profit. We make profits to run the business, to make the organization sustainable.' It's by choice. There is no compulsion. Ask yourself, what do you want? What do you want in life? You want to be rich for the next seven generations. You want an organization which will survive for the next seven generations and according to the law of attraction, whatever you give you get back in multiples. So, if you're contributing out there in the world, people will contribute in your life and if you are going to create this culture, this legacy, it will make your organization sustainable."

"Please do not misunderstand me. I asked that question out of curiosity. After all, I have come from that part of the society which is under-privileged; so I know the problems there and I certainly want to contribute and give back something to the society. Guide me in doing it, Sir," Ravi pleaded.

"There are various ways of giving it back. Some people donate for educational organizations. They work for primary education. Some of them work in the area of health. Some of them help the poor. There are so many organizations working for various causes. There are some big corporate groups; they hand over their money to certain non-government organizations. They work for the last part of the pyramid.

Yeah Ravi, as you said, you are not clear about really what to do. Really what difference to make out there in the world and how to give it back. That's what you are asking me, right?"

"Yes Sir, how?" Ravi asked.

"There are hundreds of ways. You have to decide it. If you ask me, I love to create support and nurture the entrepreneurs; as only entrepreneurs create jobs. They are able to create a certain idea, build business around that idea, and make that business big, so that they can serve more and more people. That's how they actually contribute to the GDP of the country. That's how I look at business. For that, there are various ways of contribution. This is my own way of doing it. If someone wants to be a successful entrepreneur, to be rich for the next seven generations, to make his organization sustainable for the next seven generations, I serve the entrepreneurs by giving advice. I create, support and nurture the entrepreneurs.

There are various ways of doing this. The first one is education. You can educate people. You can motivate them, you can inspire them. You actually go and meet them on one-to-one basis or you can create certain courses for them. Educate them to walk on a pathway of success, to walk on a path of richness, and to demonstrate leadership on the court. You can educate them through various seminars. You can arrange workshops for them. Ultimately they will be inspired to be ultra-rich, or to be rich. You can participate in the public programs. You can go as a speaker or as a guest speaker or as a chief speaker to various public programs.

Sometimes there may be people who are not really business people. You can talk to school students, go and inspire them. All the parents in the world want their kids to grow, learn and get a good job. You can go to the students and tell them to learn, grow and either do a job or a business. If you do this simple thing, that's also your contribution to the world. You can create more people like you who will do the same thing for the students. Go to the college students, tell them the same thing. You can go and talk to the farmers. Literate them financially so that they will make their living on their own and they will not make the suicide attempts like they are doing today.

You can create a structure to support them financially; the corporate sector takes social responsibility according to the government norms. Each organization has to put their money in certain social causes. You can create a fund for them; it will support the budding entrepreneurs in starting up their businesses.

You can write one book or many books. Writing a book will take you to the larger audience. More and more people will read your book, and books will inspire them to be an entrepreneur or to take their businesses to the next level. You can do it."

"How can I write a book?" Ravi asked.

"It's very simple. In your very first book, you can share your own story. How you were struggling earlier, and what you are doing now and what you are planning to do. If you share all this in a simple way in your book, it will inspire people.

You can take your friends who are already successful entrepreneurs with you. They will join you in this movement. You can also create all those startups you have funded. You can fund. You can create a group of entrepreneurs who will walk along with you on this same path. They may also come up with different ideas. You can serve more and more people in this way.

You can create, support and nurture all these entrepreneurs by training them. It will make a difference in this way when they are successful in their business. This way, you can pass it on, making a difference to the next seven generations. This is the very simple way of doing it.

You can guide an entrepreneur you meet in any conference or seminar; he will guide another one. If one entrepreneur can create five more entrepreneurs, then our purpose will be served." I had given away to him whatever knowledge I had.

"So," I said, "these are the main seven aspects of successful entrepreneurship."

"Sir!" Ravi exclaimed, "We can call them the Seven Sutras of successful entrepreneurship!"

"Wonderful, Ravi! Seven is a magical figure. There are seven continents in this world. A rainbow has seven colors. There are seven 'saptarshi's in the sky, there are seven 'soor's in our music, seven oceans on earth, there are seven 'janma's according to the Hindu mythology, there are seven wonders in the world, Snow White lived with seven dwarves, Sindbad the Sailor had seven voyages, James Bond has the number 007. There might be so many seven things...? When you get married, you will take those seven 'phere', we call it 'saptapadi. That is the importance of seven. That is why this figure always inspires me. My lucky number is also seven." I was also delighted.

Ravi said, "Let me list those Seven Sutras...

'The Blueprint of Entrepreneurship'.

'Fund-Raising and Financial Management'.

'Sale, Sale, Sale.'

'Leadership'.

'Building a Winning Team'.

'System of Systems'.

'Making a Difference'."

Ravi was very excited, "Thank you very much, Sir! You have truly shown me the right path. All my doubts are clear now. I feel that I am ready now to start my business afresh. But first of all, I will rush to Angel and apologize to her..."

"All my best wishes are with you, Ravi!" I said.

He went away, with new dreams in his eyes and new plans in his mind. I really wished him good luck from the bottom of my heart. I entered my cabin again. There on the table were the bottles of massage oils he had presented to me. I smiled to myself and prayed that he should not have to come to me again with some problems and dilemmas of his life… that his love story will have the happy ending…"And they lived happily ever after…"

I really wished this from the bottom of my heart…

Chapter 14

Being Ultra-Rich

Twelve years had passed after that last visit of the young man and today one Rolls Royce and one Maybach stopped in front of my house. I saw some guests coming out of the cars. And to my surprise, Ravi and his family stood at my doorstep. Now he was sitting before me, a middle-aged gentleman dressed immaculately, along with his beautiful wife and two smart kids!

"Ravi, what happened after you went from my office last time? I think it was around ten to twelve years back, right? And, yes… can I still call you 'Ravi', if you don't mind?" I asked.

"Please do not embarrass me, Sir. You have full rights to call me 'Ravi'! What I am today is because of you, Wealth Guru!" Ravi said.

"So, as I took your leave, I called Angel." He began his story of twelve years.

"I said to her, 'I want to talk to you. I met the Wealth Guru. He suggested to me so many things. I want to share them with you.' Angel said, 'I'm fed up with all your stories now. I really don't want to meet you. You just forget me and let me live my life happily. And you also live happily. My best wishes are with you.' Then I said, 'Angel, please listen to me. We'll meet only for three to four hours. This can be our last meeting or this meeting will make us life partners."

She laughed loudly over the phone and said, 'Life partners? Forget about that. But, okay… let us meet for the last time. I'm ready.' Then I went to her home in Mumbai and I shared with her everything that you had told me. Initially for half an hour, she was not really listening. I am trained in how to listen to people and how to make others to listen to me. I used all my skills, as I did not want to lose her. I told her, 'See Angel, you are really worried that I am unable to give you time, right? That's the major concern you have. Right now, I'm not giving you time. How will I behave in the future and how will I be a good family man; that's the main concern you have. Is that right? If I'm not giving time right now to my girlfriend, then how will I give time to my wife or my kids? I can understand your concern. But please listen to me.'

And I shared all the seven sutras you taught me. After listening to it Angel got overwhelmed and said, 'Wow, this is awesome! My father is my mentor but he has not taught me such things. He has only trained me in making more money and other stuff. Though he's my father, he's my mentor also. He's my business Guru. But, this is really new and this is really awesome. This will really work Ravi.' And then she changed her mind and consented to get married to me. She said, 'I trust you Ravi; I hope you will stick to these seven sutras. Moreover I trust your Wealth Guru; he seems to be really influential. I want to meet him some day.' I promised her that I would take her to meet you. After that, we celebrated. We had a party at the 'Taj Lands End'.

Then we decided to meet daily for a month. We met in the evenings at various venues and spent time together. After the month passed, I asked Angel, 'Now, we should decide about our future; what do you think?'

She said, 'Ravi! Now, I am clear about whatever you have shared with me and I like the way you shared everything with me. I'm observing you since last month. I see a major shift in your way of thinking and in your way of acting. Really, I am very happy. I can see that you can create really big things in life and this will lead to the business empire of your dreams. I am confident about that. I am really in a hurry to go to Mama and Papa to share all this with them, as I have told them earlier about us. I have also shared all that happened with us in between. I don't know how Papa will react to this. Mama is always on my side, but you don't know my father. He is a professional hunter and he is very possessive about me. He always has two guns in his bedroom. I don't know how he will react to all this, but let us go and see.'

She then said, 'I am in a real hurry to go and meet my parents and share with them. I want to marry you now, so no issues. I'll marry you even if they would not agree. But, if it happens with their consent, especially with my father's, I'll be the happiest woman on this planet. Why not to go to Spain then and meet them? Let us go to Barcelona!'

Then we completed the formalities, visa, etc. on my side, as fast as we could. I booked tickets with the Elite Airways. We had booked First Class tickets. We had flat-bed seats and stylish kit bags that included luxury Italian brand Bvlgari fragrances and lotions. We dined from Royal Doulton bone china plates with exclusive Robert Welch cutlery. It was truly a dream flight!

As we entered Barcelona, the first thing that struck me was the climate. It was warm and pleasant like any sea shore city. I saw many architectural beauties along the road to Angel's house. I had read that Barcelona is famous for its

Gothic architecture and I had an immense interest in it. We had planned to visit some sites during our trip.

We reached Angel's parents' home; it was royal! Her parents welcomed both of us. After having some rest and refreshment in the evening, all of us sat together to have some wine before dinner. At that time, the subject of marriage came up. Angel's Papa asked me, 'In which airlines did you come from India?' I said, 'Elite Airways.' He looked at me with surprise and said, 'Ooh… Elite! Yeah, in this season, some good offers are also going on with them. That is fine. In which class did you come?' I said calmly, 'We both came in First Class.' He was again surprised to hear that and said, 'What do you say? You are not joking?' I again said, 'Yes, we came in the First Class.' He said, 'Really! That is great! I wonder how you could afford it!" I could not comprehend his meaning. Was he contemptuous or was he insulting me? I decided to say a word or two to him; but at that moment I looked at Angel. She was watching me with a pleading expression on her face. I calmed down a bit. I realized that if I do not want to lose her; I should retain my calm. I should control myself.

Angel rushed to my rescue. She interrupted our conversation and said, 'Papa, Ravi is totally changed. He has transformed himself. I am observing him for the last ten days. He is a new guy now. I'm sure that he will create a really big business empire and I want to marry him, no matter what may happen. Papa, I know that you'll agree with our proposal, as you love me most in this world.' Her Papa smiled and left us, making an excuse. Her mother also went in with him. She might have discussed with him about us and convinced him. They came after some time and declared that they would give consent to our marriage on one condition. Her father said, 'I have one condition, both of you are going to be life partners but you have separate businesses. Why not to be business partners first? Angel, dear, as I am your mentor, I think that from business perspective, this will be a win-win for both of you. This is my suggestion, and I will agree to this proposal of marriage if both of you merge your business entities. I don't want anything from Angel's business or your business, I have sufficient amount of money with me. I have my business to take care of me. I have set up such a structure, so I don't want anything from you. But, I wish that the wedding should be in Indian style and a Mega-Indian wedding. Angel's Mama will also be very happy. Arrange it in India, so I'll come along with my relatives and friends.' I was so happy that I said 'yes' to his every proposal!

I will tell all other happenings very shortly. I talked to my parents and relatives about all the arrangements and we all decided the venue to be in Udaipur in Rajasthan. It was truly a grand Indian wedding. We chose the famous Jagmandir Palace as the venue. It is often referred to as a swarg ki vatika or garden of heaven. It was a three-day wedding with cocktails, theme-dinners, banquets and wedding ceremonies. The fresh flowers and special lighting, folk dancers and fireworks brought alive this garden of heaven in vibrant colors of celebrations. Musical soirees and performances were organized at the Garden Courtyard, wedding ceremonies at Kunwarpada Chowk, lavish buffets and sit-down banquets at Kunwarpada Lawns. The Indian media did a lot of coverage of it. It was the biggest three-phased marriage which happened in the last few years.

I had called you to invite you for the ceremony, but your phone was not reachable for quite some days," Ravi said.

"Yes Ravi, I was out of India for a month," I said.

"I wish you could attend it... This one wish of mine remained unfulfilled..." Ravi complained.

"Such things happen, Ravi. I do not need to tell you," I said.

Ravi started talking again, "The marriage fever lasted for fifteen days! Then slowly we went back to work. Angel was already doing business in Mumbai, Delhi, Chennai, Bengaluru and Singapore. She knew people there. She had contacts. We merged our two entities 'Angel Developers and Ravi associates', it has become RANGEL realtors. After the merger, Rangel realtors decided to list it on the National Stock Exchange. We started the planning for the IPO. After creating a team of advisors, hot discussions about the new board members went on for eight days. After eight days of further discussion, brainstorming and all that, we came to a conclusion that one cousin brother of mine, who is serving Shell corporation as well as one friend of Angel who is an architect from Delhi, will join the board. We formed the board of four. There was one more vacant position which we decided to fill later. This way, the IPO got really a big hit. And we shifted to the very upper domain of business world."

"That was really a good move Ravi," I said.

"The real story of Rangel starts now, Sir," Ravi said.

We had been chatting for quite some time now. My wife had arranged a hearty breakfast and I invited Ravi and his family to it. We rose and went to the dining room.

Chapter 15

Conquering the Seven Continents

After having the breakfast, Ravi resumed his success story.

"After creating the initial capital from the global expansion, the board along with the advisors sat together and prepared a business plan according to the board's advice. We decided to create a business plan of seven years along with certain milestones of five years, three years and one year. There was already a real estate sector. Along with that, we decided to enter in the hospitality sector. From Angel's creative mind, an idea came up, why not to think about hospitality sector too? Real estate and hospitality will go hand in hand. I said, 'Okay, if you like it, then you please take this business in your portfolio.'"

"Then the board decided to go in three businesses basically. Already the Rangel realtors were working in the real estate city development. Then we decided to go in the hospitality sector too, creating the resorts and some city hotels. Angel's dream was to create resorts globally, actually, in all the seven continents," Ravi said smilingly.

"She is truly a visionary," I appreciated.

"The board gave consent to that," Ravi continued. "I told Angel to manage the entities, the Rangel realtors as well as the Rangel hospitality. I always used to share your

Sutras with her and she always had them in mind. She was fascinated with the words 'Think Big'!"

She is a visionary as you said, Sir. She has new ideas coming up every day. One day she came to me and said, 'How about this new concept of 'Island Living'? I was very excited to hear her plans. She has the entrepreneurship in her blood. We prepared a blueprint and started working on it. She started to buy islands all over the world and created a model of Island Living. 'Get younger and live longer' was her tagline for this project. She received the famous award 'Island Queen' for this project.

Initially, some orthodox countries didn't encourage the idea; but the liberal countries upheld this. We already had acquaintances with many Prime Ministers, Presidents and Sultans of many countries. They liked this project and introduced it to their contacts and networks.

I was very pleased to hear the story. I said, "I congratulate both of you!"

Ravi said, "There is another story, sir! As you know, I love nature and naturopathy is very dear to me and Ayurveda is my real passion. Ayurveda is the real remedy which acts on the root cause of any disease or any health ailments. So, we decided to start Rangel Ayurveda too!"

"We named it 'RavirVeda!'" Angel said with a smile.

Ravi said, "Sir, I have launched and promoted RavirVeda according to your Seven Sutras."

"First of all Angel and I prepared a blueprint for this business. While doing this the picture of next seven years became clear to me and I prepared an action-plan in that line and started to follow it. I reached RavirVeda's break-even in one year because of that.

After creating the blueprint Angel and I did brainstorming and finalized our plan. We set up a structure of meetings of all the board members and advisers. I did not open my own factory for this purpose; instead I decided the standards and contents of my product and registered them under my brand. I procured my product from other manufacturers; as per your teaching 'Earning money without investing a single penny'. My team is certainly a winning team. I always remember your words 'The best HR management in the world is to love people.' I follow that religiously. I really love all my team members. I take care of them. I innovate new strategies to give them comfort of high level. I spend a lot of money on their training and development every year.

I use all the latest technologies for financial management. I write down my personal expenditure every night as you had told me. My wife Angel, Vardhan and Jolly also do the same thing. Your saying in this matter always inspires me; 'Accounting and investments are two specialties of people who become rich.' In my profession too, I followed this principle. I had weekly meetings with my accounts head. I used to meet my company secretary, chartered accountant every month and took their advice. People rush to their C.A. at the year ending. I think this is foolish behavior; you had said so. I benefitted by your advice to meet my C.A. and company secretary every month and discussed innovative ways of doing business with them regularly and implemented their advice." Ravi said.

"Good!" I exclaimed.

"I have very cordial relationship with my investors. That is why; they give useful information to me about investments. I have shifted in the investor category because of their contact and my passive income increased tremendously. I have money available to me to start any project anytime. I learnt investment skills from them and invested in small companies. Now those have become a big name.

I appointed Mr. Robert Braganza as my mentor for this new business. He has launched and owns a world famous brand of pharmacy and beauty-care products. He help me to promote RavirVeda all over the world."

I said, "I am really proud of you. You have truly implementing all the principles which I taught you."

Ravi, "Yes Sir, there are many other things. I find half an hour in a week for myself and think rigorously. I ponder over the current situation, whether RavirVeda requires my guidance in some department. And if I find such a thing, I appoint a new leader for that purpose and train him accordingly. By doing this, my business runs on an automatic mode. Sir, what you had said has become true. I only concentrated mainly on leadership and management and today I am a very successful entrepreneur.

The sales team of my company is very hard-working. I gain energy and enthusiasm from them. My company still uses your formulas for selling the products. 20% of RavirVeda's products are such that 80% of people use them and 80% products are such that 20% of people of certain class use them. We launched our each and every product in an innovative way. That is why people are still curious about our new product, though there are 257 products of RavirVeda. We not only sell a product, we sell a new thought- 'Embrace nature and stay fit.' That is the reason, people demand our products. We always make sure before launching any product that it gives more value than its price. Our sales persons are confident that we give something more valuable than its price every time.

I have been able to do all these things because of a proper system. I have a certain system for manufacturing and selling my products. I have appointed new consultants to implement this system and my company has become world famous because of this system. My systems include purchase system, production system, quality control system, billing system, dispatch system, sales system, distributing systems and I am completely free from all the workload.

In this way, RavirVeda is doing fine and I implemented same Sutras in Rangel also. Now, I have enough money for my next seven generations."

"I am truly amazed by your story Ravi! I have rarely come across a man like you in my whole life," I said.

"Sir, I want to tell you something more. As I had told you before, I was always concerned about the living of Indian people," Ravi said, "Some impure ghee replaced pure desi ghee in my childhood. Since then I am against this overuse of chemicals in our life. Everyday bath soap too contains chemicals. Indians and human beings all over the world got trapped in this vicious circle. That is why I started my first business in Ayurvedic hair oil, as Ayurvedic products have lesser side-effects. I did the real-estate business for survival, but my real passion was Ayurveda. I appointed R & D team to search for the defects in that oil. We came up with the slogan 'Swadeshi' for our products. I studied the Charak Sanhita and many old manuscripts of Ayurveda. We created many products containing Aloe Vera, Neem, Tulsi etc. This time I shifted the whole approach. We decided to create my image as a brand of Ayurveda. I published the materials on Web, in the seminars, in the workshops, in the public speaking programs and in the writing blogs of Ayurveda. As you know my love for Ayurveda, I gave free samples of that magic hair oil of my grandma created from my grandma's secret formula. I gave those free samples everywhere. Throughout India, I spoke about Ayurveda and the benefits of Ayurveda.

We, I mean my organization started encouraging farmers to produce herbs. I am giving a good price to all the raw materials without compromising in quality, keeping the price very competitive and affordable to any human being. This strategy works like anything sir."

We held awareness campaigns and the sell increased. I noticed that and concentrated more on awareness programs. People started demanding more variety and we created a vast range of products from shampoos to beauty products, varieties of hair oil etc. We captured half of the national market."

"So, you achieved your unfinished mission of hair-oil production; that is great!" I said.

"Yes Sir!" Ravi smiled. "Moreover, we started a separate branch for Ayurvedic medicinal products. I searched for young entrepreneurs, men and women form small villages and towns and made models for the franchise. The brand 'RavirVeda' won the whole national market. The first overseas demand came from the NRIs from the UK, South Africa and the Gulf countries. We set up stores there and then started the production also. We took help from the natural native herbs and plants of countries like China, Thailand and Indonesia and made combinations with our Indian herbs to make new products. Angel's network helped us immensely in doing this. Many countries that had banned the Ayurvedic products earlier started to buy them from us.

"Ravi is known as 'Yogacharya' and 'Ayurvedacharya' and promotes Yoga in more than 100 countries," Angel said.

"We have offices in London, Johannesburg, Singapore and Amsterdam," Ravi continued.

"Where are you settled now?" I asked.

"We decided to settle down in Amsterdam as the city has geographical benefits. It is a good city to live, has a good culture and a safe place. We have built a eco-friendly house there. I remembered your Rajasthani style house, while building it. We have named it 'VarJolly' after our kids! You must visit it anytime you wish. We will be more than happy to extend our hospitality towards you! We have achieved all this because of you Sir!" Ravi said.

"You had your passion Ravi, that is why you have achieved all this," I said.

"Thanks for your kind words, sir. We have printed the Seven Sutras and placed them in our offices. My desktop and my laptop screensaver have those sutras. Angel has conquered the seven oceans, and the seven continents. Now, Rangel hospitality is a big brand, and Rangel 7 star resorts are known worldwide.

"You have implemented my teachings very effectively. I am proud of you Ravi!" I said and I meant it.

"I got retired two years back. Three years back, Angel retired. At present, we do something if we wish to, otherwise we enjoy. As Angel got retired first, she initiated your formula of making difference. I too am working on education: the incubation, public speaking, the funding and all those seven sutras. I am helping to create more entrepreneurs like me, which is your dream and I am contributing to it. You can say, I am paying my 'Guru Dakshina' in this way!" Ravi said.

"And what is there in that parcel?" I asked. I looked at the big box he gave me few hours ago when all of them came inside.

"Sir, it is a small gift from us. They are the 257 products of RavirVeda," Ravi said."

"Oh! Thank you so much Ravi," I received the gift with delight.

"We want to thank you sir from the bottom of our hearts!" he said.

I hugged him tightly.

So many people came, took my advice and left. I have heard countless stories of success and failures. But this story touched my heart. This man came, took my advice but did not leave my heart. His was the story which was to remain there forever...

THE END